HOW TO BE A BEACON IN A DARK WORLD

Every Soul Matters

◆ ◆ ◆

PAUL DILLOW

HOW TO BE A BEACON IN A DARK WORLD

ISBN: 9781799210986

REVIEWS

There are some books that encourage, challenge, and move you closer to Christ and this is one of those books! I have the honor of knowing the Dillow family and I pray that my family will have the same passion as his family for the things of God. Paul Dillow opens up about his life and the providential leading of God. You will experience Paul and Linda being in the palms of the Lord's hands as He leads them through each stage of life. Their story will take you to your story to seeing the goodness of God's plan in all of your life. What a reassurance knowing that God is at work in all of life circumstances. The journey of Paul and Linda will give you practical help in raising a family and encourage you that in every season of life God has a purpose. This season of life for Paul and Linda is leading the member care team at First Baptist Daytona Beach and they are the BEST! This book will give you and your church practical steps to care for each member because every soul matters. Enjoy reading because you will be blessed!

----- *Pastor Eric Stitts, Senior Pastor, First Baptist Church of Daytona Beach*

Pastor Paul Dillow's book *How to be a Beacon in a Dark World* is a must read for anyone aspiring to be a leader in a local congregation or desiring to begin a Pastoral Care Ministry.

God's providential hand is evidenced through this semi-autobiographical overview of Pastor Dillow's life. Fifty years in ministry has yielded experience from both sides of the pulpit. The reader will glean nuggets of wisdom reaped from a life of ministry involving leadership, a vibrant prayer life, God's providence and skills required to develop a Member Care Ministry.

Pastor Paul liberally uses scripture to validate his words of wisdom. He presents his material using humor making this an enjoyable and inspirational reading experience.

----- *Dr. Charles Harrell, Ormond Beach, FL*

Pastor Paul has interwoven his providentially driven life story with foundational biblical truths, a refreshing examination of the church and its ministries, and with passionate call for a regeneration of a specific ministry area. Pastor Paul speaks, writes and serves in a very honest, humble, transparent, captivating manner. Any reader will find his unique writing style, infused with metaphors, illustrations and witticisms, to be refreshing and enjoyable. He writes like he talks and what he writes is what he lives, as evidence of who he is in Christ.

You will find the book, from its seemingly simple beginning as an enjoyable, peaceful biographical story, transforms increasingly into an informative teaching and encouragement story, and then crescendos into a passionate, preaching, call-to-action story. I felt like I had gone to church.

Finally, Pastor Paul's call for churches to move purposely from predominantly a Pastoral Care Paradigm into predominantly a Member Care Paradigm is biblical and essential for church and the individual Christian health and growth.

Read this book. I laughed and I cried. I was moved and encouraged. And, yes I was changed. I pray that you, your ministry and your church will be too.

----- *Mr. Thomas Moss, Port Orange, FL*

Dear Reader,

The genuine Christian is one who is true in his soul and in his life. Others clearly see the evidence in his life and behavior. They hear the proof from his mouth. The genuine believer testifies that Christ is his Savior and Lord; and he is totally committed to serving only Him. Jesus Christ is the foundation of all he believes. Ask him for the hope that is within him and he will answer, "It is the life, the death, and the resurrection of his Lord and Master". Christ is my hope in this life and the life to come. My earnest prayer is that He is your hope as well.

1 Peter 3:15 "But sanctify the Lord God in your hearts, and always be ready to give a defense to everyone who asks you a reason for the hope that is in you, with meekness and fear." NKJV

Dedication

Linda Dillow,
My wife, my friend, my ministry partner.
Your love, encouragement and patience are matchless.

Acknowledgements

When I count the blessings in my life, family tops the list. In the early years, my parents and two wonderful sisters, Gail & Sandra, showered my path with encouragement.

A bit later, my wife and two sons, David & Darin, made the journey easy, enjoyable and worth the effort.

Our daughter-in-law, Bethany, has made our journey very special. The icing on the cake are the grandchildren and recently the addition of great grandchildren.
Our church LifeGroup, fellow Member Care team partners, fellow pastors and church family supply day to day encouragement, prayers and support.

Special thanks to Dr. Charles Harrell and his wife Anna and Thom Moss and his wife Karen for their contributions to this effort.

Last but not least, a thank you to Pastor Eric Stitts for his constant support and encouragement.

WE ARE TRULY BLESSED.

CONTENTS

INTRODUCTION

"HOW TO BE A BEACON IN A DARK WORLD"

Matthew 20:27-28
"And whoever desires to be first among you,
let him be your slave,
just as the Son of Man did not come to be served,
but to serve,
and to give His life a ransom for many." NKJV

A journey begins with the first step. For example, this book represents my first attempt at writing and may be the last. Confession is good for the soul. God gives us threescore and ten years on this planet and even that is not a guarantee. So, having raced significantly past that mile mark, there is nothing to gain by pretense.

My spiritual journey began at the age of ten and will be complete when I see Jesus. But for now, a mid-journey senior moment has taken pole position in this race.

There are numerous examples of senior moments: forgetting names or where you parked your car in the supermarket lot to name a couple. My personal senior moment is the decision to become an author at the advanced age of beyond seventy, which is something totally out of this man's comfort zone. However, God revealed a need.

Every right-minded individual seems to be searching for ways to live a genuine and meaningful life. All well intended people want to live a life with purpose and a life that is genuine or real. Let's face it, this world is full of actors, make believe people, and people without real purpose, going nowhere and accomplishing nothing more than self-gratification. There is more to life than such a shallow self-serving existence.

I decided to let my light shine!

This little light of mine,

I'm gonna let it shine

This little light of mine,

I'm gonna let it shine

This little light of mine,

I'm gonna let it shine

Let it shine, let it shine,

let it shine [1]

So, Why Write This Book?

Sensing a need through providential encounters, God placed on my heart a deep desire to answer the call. An inner voice whispered and said, "make yourself available; there is a work for you to do". The answer was, yes Lord; and He supernaturally opened many doors and led in a powerful way.

God gave me the desire to share my spiritual journey to encourage others to look beyond themselves. The prerequisite for finding genuineness and meaning in life is to first search internally. Ensuring a personal relationship with God is an absolute must for finding meaning and purpose in life. An encounter with Jesus, God's Son, is the first step. Without Jesus in your heart, you will always be searching, but never discovering your purpose.

For the Christian, each experience is a teacher. This book includes relevant applications to better relay spiritual insight from those experiences. Also included are references to certain people that God placed strategically along the way to providentially carry out His purpose. I've omitted actual names to protect the innocent and the guilty as well.

The purpose of this book is twofold. First, it is my sincere desire that you will find Jesus. And going forward, that you discover the path to a genuine and meaningful life. You can be a beacon in this dark world.

It is NOT the purpose of this book to elevate the author to a level of self-proclaimed expert on any of the subject matter covered within its pages. There have been failures along the way as well as blessings. The failures are mostly a result of my doing and the blessings all come from God. I take no credit.

Sadly, most people live for self. Frequently, it is not

until the autumn of life that the focus shifts from self to others. Just like you, I am a work in progress.

If the reading of this book results in a destiny change or a priority change in just one person, the effort has been more than worth it. It is my view and God's as well, that "every soul matters".

PART ONE - THE NEED IDENTIFIED

John 4:35 “Do you not say,
'There are still four months and then comes
the harvest'? Behold, I say to you,
lift up your eyes and look at the fields,
for they are already white for harvest!” NKJV

Opportunities to serve the Lord abound. You will find them in every city, at every intersection, every street corner and at every crossroad in life. However, other distractions often blind us. Without argument, we are living in a very self-centered society. Everyone wants his own way and to do his own thing. The message, "hey look at me", jumps out at us from multiple media sources twenty-four hours a day.

Despite the distractions, it has been my personal experience, that God is constantly working, providentially, in our lives to bring us, first, into a personal relationship with Him. He then desires that we reach a level of full spiritual maturity. He wants to teach us that it is not about us, rather, it's all about Him.

SECTION I - OPEN HEART SURGERY

◆ ◆ ◆

PRE-OP PREPARATION

The Great Physician

Supernaturally saved at the age of ten, God's indwelling Holy Spirit gave me a deep desire to share my new-found faith. However, that spiritual moment of salvation did not immediately come with a desire to serve in any form of church ministry. Like the children of Israel, there were several years of wilderness wandering. Gradually, God began to change all of that.

According to King David, God knew us when we were nothing more than mere substance in the initial stages of development in our mothers' wombs. Long before we were conceived, God knew us and had a plan for our surrendered lives.

It should be no surprise that God chose our parents either, through natural means or through adoption. With God, there are no mistakes. He has a plan and a purpose for each of us.

God blessed both my wife and me with great parents. My parents never encouraged participation in sports; however, they more than encouraged participation in church-related activities. In fact, participation was mandatory unless there was a deathbed experience, or so it seemed. My two wonderful older sisters were always present to ensure that participation. Just to say that I am thankful for a Godly family would be a huge understatement. It was a blessing beyond measure.

During the fifties, most considered the Boy Scouts of America, at least in our small town, a church connected organization. The Boy Scouts of America organization was all about God and country. A big plus, dad was a scout leader. The Boy Scout slogan and the Boy Scout motto were both meant for character building. Field activities taught cooperation and team building. God was slowly changing his new servant one providential step at a time.

Still being a bit self-centered, a lot of work remained to prepare this soul for ministry. Around the age of fifteen, another providential encounter occurred. My pastor encouraged involvement in the Boy Scouts of America's God and Country Award. He and his wife led me through the process. Both this pastor and his wife had a profound influence on my life. They emphasized this truth:

Our country was founded on Christian principles, and if called on, every Christian should be willing to serve and even fight to defend those principles.

Their clear and lasting message was that service to country was a Christian responsibility. That message left a mark.

But there were still plenty of excuses remaining for

not getting involved in church work. There were age, qualification, and spiritual maturity factors to consider before taking on a ministry or church work of any kind. Later, but not yet.

My attitude: Church work was for the older folks. Church work was a job for the pastors, deacons, trustees, or the women's groups. There were more important things to do with the time. Thank God He was, and is, a patient God.

Another providential encounter occurred at the age of seventeen while working at a local service station in my hometown. A car entered the service lane next to where I was working. A beautiful young lady sat in the backseat of her parent's car. Our eyes met, we each smiled and, to make a long story short, that was fifty-seven years ago. And now with two sons, nine grandchildren, and three great-grandchildren the smiles are still there.

We were married a few years later. It just didn't happen that I married someone with a caring heart, it was providential, and it was God's plan. He chose us to be a ministry team.

But family plans stalled for a time. God had more training in store - basic training. Out of love for country, the United States Air Force would be second in command for the next four years. My wife and I lived in England for a couple of years allowing us the experience of living in a different culture and among diverse types of people. As a nuclear weapons technician, God was teaching me the value of teamwork. He was also teaching self-discipline; while also teaching both of us patience and trust.

After the military experience, my wife and I moved into our first home near our old home town. We started attending a local church where my wife experienced the next providential, better said, supernatural encounter.

My wife had always been a good and a very caring person; but she was not a professing Christian. However, continuing prayer, the Word, and the convicting power of the Holy Spirit changes people. It wasn't long until she also accepted God's gift of salvation. We were now truly a team. It was undoubtedly providential preparation.

God is Watching and So Are Your Children

If you want your children to have the best chance for finding a genuine and meaningful life, the effort begins with you. First, parents must set the example. Second, church attendance must be established as a non-optional weekly event with your entire family. Twice a year appearance sends a loud and clear message to your children that God is not that important.

Embracing a non-rebellious deep respect for your country, its leaders and those who enforce its laws is more than idealistic, God requires it.

1 Peter 2:13-14 "Submit yourselves for the Lord's sake to every authority instituted among men: whether to the king, as the supreme authority, or to governors, who are sent by him to punish those who do wrong and to commend those who do right" NKJV

Respect is an essential building block for finding meaning and purpose in life.

Finding meaning in life and learning how to be genuine is a process. The process often takes many twists and turns. When we belong to Jesus, we are not in charge. He is constantly working to sand off the rough edges and pound out the dents.

Never underestimate the power of prayer. ***Prayer changes situations and changes people.*** Praying for God to reveal to you the purpose for your life is an absolute necessity. He has a work for you to do, but you need to ask for the revelation.

Surrounded by Genuine People

I'll make a bold statement, ***"life begins with your parents".***

After that obvious conclusion and more to the point, my spiritual journey began, principally, because of Godly parents. My church attendance started while still in my mother's womb.

After a grand entrance, this same Godly lady was always reciting scripture to me and singing "Jesus Loves Me, This I Know, for the Bible Tells Me So."[2]

Again, two older sisters helped me toe the line as well. They reported any occasional unacceptable actions to the Commander in Chief - mom. I still think that painful paddling after my fight with another young boy in the stairwell of the church was unnecessary.

My father, (Sunshine), on the other hand, taught the practical side of life. In those early training years, dad taught lawn mowing, taking out trash, and other unique and useful skills. At the age of seven, dad had me on the roof of our two-story home teaching me how to install shingles. This wonderful person also taught me how to fish and enjoy the great outdoors. His experience as a riverboat pilot on the Ohio River fascinated me. Listening to those old stories, time and time again, never grew old.

DAD'S RIVER BOAT - 1937

My wife was a God send. Her support was and is tireless. As a life and ministry partner, she has been supportive through every minute of this journey. Her advice always comes in the form of positive suggestions. Learning is much more than hearing, it involves listening as well. We are truly a team. We have petitioned our heavenly Father, that He quietly take us home together at an advanced age, so long as we still are useful in ministry.

Your Life Makes A Difference

The pastor of our local church in those early years loved children. He took time to listen and to mentor. I was able to multitask at an early age and attention to his sermons supplied a lot of direction.

The Junior High Sunday School teacher at church was loving, patient and extremely tolerant, even after our class of mischievous boys locked him in the classroom for the entire length of the morning Worship Service. Yes, there was a slight personal role in that activity. Other Sunday School teachers were not always so tolerant. A curious mind at times tested their patience. However, I didn't consider turning a foam fire extinguisher upside down and watching the contents discharge and cover the entire class, including a certain teacher, that big of a deal. Lesson learned after a brief suspension from Sunday School - not every adult is equally tolerant.

Two older men in our church caught my attention. They both just seemed so spiritual, so close to the Lord. Were they authentic or just putting on a show? They were, in fact, very genuine. One of them prayed with me that Sunday morning when I gave my life to Christ. The other, a business owner, arranged my first job in my teen years. They were indeed genuine.

Providential people came in many varieties during my four years spent in the military. First, there was the Sergeant at the basic training facility in Texas. He taught diligence, when he assigned me the task of scrubbing the cracks in the floor of the barracks with a toothbrush. Later in my military career, another Sergeant taught me better driving skills, after my accident on a forklift. God had to be watching over this forklift operator on that day.

I believe God's sovereignty is all inclusive. No one is outside of His providential control whether they accept it or not. He does control nations and even unbelieving people to accomplish His purpose. However, satan still rules the hearts of unbelievers.

2 Cor. 4:4 "In their case the god of this world has blinded the minds of the unbelievers, to keep them from seeing the light of the gospel of the glory of Christ who is the image of God." NKJV

SOME GOLDEN DAYBREAK JESUS WILL COME

A YOUNG HEART

A Youthful View

During my adolescent years, I paid little attention to older adults except, of course, my parents. Most adults just seemed so old. Grade-school teachers were older than dirt, or so they appeared. The Sunday School teachers and most of the youth leaders at church seemed old as well.

Looking back, there was obviously a youthful unawareness of the fact that ***no one escapes life's inevitable cycles.*** In youth, there was a failure to fully recognize or embrace the unique contributions of the older generation. That would change over time. Don't misinterpret, I always treated elders with respect. My parents would have it no other way.

God, in his providential ways, would eventually move to close that generation gap to prepare both of us for our future ministry with adults and a later ministry with senior adults - little did we know.

I've devoted a substantial portion of the remainder of this book to that final phase of this ministry journey

- Member Care. However, only God knows for certainty what the final ministry calling will be. Another need coupled with another journey may yet materialize.

The next providential event would prove to be the beginning of our ministry journey together. This God orchestrated opportunity appeared in our early twenties. My wife and I were enjoying the worship and fellowship at our local church. God was blessing the church with new converts weekly. Entire families were joining; children and teens were coming out of the woodwork.

Young people, particularly teenagers, were welcome company to both myself and my wife. There seemed to be a lot of common ground. Everything does seem to have its season. The Senior Pastor of the church noticed our love and concern for these teenagers and young people. No doubt, God was using this pastor to move us into ministry. The pastor asked if we would pray about serving as youth leaders at the church. "Wow" was our response. Trembling and fear struck us both. In fact, fear drove us to our knees. God revealed a need and we answered the call.

God blessed this ministry in a mighty way. The youth group grew to over seventy teens in just a few months. They came from all walks of life. Some came from broken homes, while others came from strong Christian families. They came from everywhere and we loved them all equally. Some students went on to become pastors and others became missionaries. Still others became great parents and remained in the same area.

Our church eventually joined a national christian youth program. Our teen group was able to take part in basketball marathons, and in many other multi-church activities. It was a very personal spiritual growth time for everyone involved.

At the time, I had a fear of praying in public, much less speaking in public. With God's help, I overcame both in time. On the humorous side in one morning service, the pastor unknowingly called on me to pray no less than four times. By the fourth prayer, I was down to two or three words - Dear Jesus and Amen. I believe God does have a sense of humor.

It was during a multi-church basketball marathon that I won my first soul to Christ. The speaker preached the gospel message and gave an invitation. I was a volunteer counselor trying to hide behind the other counselors. However, teens responded to the invitation in droves. The speaker called for all counselors, including me. A young boy by the name of Bill came to me. The two of us went outside, and, with the help of the Holy Spirit, I used the book of Romans to lead Bill to Christ.

It was a moment that changed Bill's life and mine. Little did I know at the time, God was preparing me for the gospel ministry.

The need among teenagers during that period for spiritual influence and guidance was huge. Negative forces were at work in a mighty way during the decade of the late sixties. Many of today's liberal leaders in our country, unfortunately, grew up during that time.

Yes, the need for spiritual influence was great. My wife and I answered the call. Our youth ministry experience resulted in spiritual growth for both of us and for the students as well. The ministry truly brought purpose and meaning to our life. It was a genuine God inspired experience.

Disciples Make Disciples

Although youth ministry is a big part of today's church structure, there is no biblical reference specifically for youth ministry. However, sound biblical principles can be the foundation for such ministries in the church. Sadly, too many youth ministries embrace the latest fads. All student ministries should follow the same biblical principles as any other ministry in the church.

God gave us the principles for all ministry in the Scriptures. The objective should be, not just to grow a youth group, but to see biblical convictions and commitment replicated in the lives of the teens.

Every church ministry's goal should be to make disciples. Youth ministry should be no different. Youth ministry should be both active and spiritual. Youth ministry, and others, should follow the model in *2 Timothy.*

2 Timothy 3:16-17 "Scripture is given by inspiration of God, and is profitable for doctrine, for reproof, for correction, for instruction in righteousness, that the man of God may be complete, thoroughly equipped for every good work." NKJV

Mentoring students in character building, instructing them in doctrine, and equipping them for every good work equips students for future ministry. ***Youth leaders should also model, mentor, and equip students in Christ-like behavior.*** They will do as you do, not always as you say. According to many historians on the life of Christ, about half of His original disciples were teens when He began His discipling ministry. One could argue that Jesus was the original youth leader.

The goal for every youth leader should be to make disciples that results in the unleashing of the power of God in

their lives. Teens are at the place in their lives where they need to know God's truth, how to live a God centered life, and what God's desire is for their life.

Real & Genuine Teenagers

The teens in our early ministry work, and their parents in many cases, were powerful influencers in our spiritual development. One young man is a Baptist pastor today. This young teen was the least likely to eventually become a pastor. Little did we know that we were mentoring and leading future church leaders. One young lady in our group, in later years, developed an incurable cancer. The disease, after a lengthy battle, took her life. The way she biblically conducted herself during her challenge amazed everyone around her and was a testimony to her strong faith. We had grown close to these young Christians.

A HEALTHY BALANCE

Balancing Ministry, Family, Vocation & School

All my ministry opportunities and/or endeavors have been of a bivocational nature. As a youth leader, balancing ministry, family responsibility, and work requirements was no easy task. Our first son was born in 1969. He was, and still is, a special gift from God. He is father to four of our grandchildren and grandfather to three of our great-grandchildren. Young boys are energetic and need a lot of care. Our son was no different.

Working as a supervisor at a local steel mill, that operated around the clock and 365 days a year, required constant on call status. This vocation required response to problems at all hours of the night. Trial and error soon revealed that if I gave God the priority at the start of each day, the way to meet all other work and family responsibilities was possible.

Also discovered was the absolute assurance that God was protecting my footsteps. On numerous occasions at the steel mill, this mortal life was in danger with a direct involvement in two plant explosions. The first event occurred on a Christmas day when called to the plant to check out a suspected gas leak. An inspection revealed the leak to be quite expansive and dangerous.

Working with another gentlemen, the attempts to stop the leak failed. I made the decision to evacuate the area in case of an explosion. After taking just a few steps, the gas line exploded knocking both of us to the ground. As a result, I broke my Timex watch, but we were otherwise okay. God was guarding our footsteps. His timing and control are always perfect. The other gentleman remarked, "I am glad you are a Christian man".

The second explosion, occurring several years later, had more sobering results. A 200-foot combustion stack near one of the plants operating units suddenly blew up and came tumbling down nearly missing several workers in the area. During an effort to secure the area after the explosion to prevent further damage, I placed my left hand in a pinch point of a valve that resulted in the loss of a part of my left ring finger. It could have been much worse. The experience taught me some valuable lessons. Life is very fragile and truly short. More importantly, God was watching over the entire situation. He had a plan. God never wastes a hurt.

Realizing that the vocation chosen was extremely dangerous, I prayed continually for God to supply something a bit safer. God supplied a way and the time to attend night classes at a local university and eventually complete an undergraduate degree. If we answer the call, God always supplies a way. He gives us strength for the journey.

God gives each person certain ministry capacities. Some people can manage a huge plate full, while others only a thimble full. In those early ministry years, and with God's help, it was full plate mode seven days a week.

As stated earlier, all my ministries had been of a bivocational nature. There are a couple of reasons for that decision: First, an observation of too many pastors fleecing the flock and second, the authority and example of God's Word. The Apostle Paul States in *1 Cor 9:18*:

"What is my reward then? That when I preach the gospel, I may present the gospel of Christ without charge, that I may not abuse my authority in the gospel." NKJV

Praise God, He eventually provided a secular identity that allowed opportunity to take His message into the workplace. At the time of God's calling, I was serving in the safety department at a local steel mill and my schedule well suited my ministry. More importantly, this vocation in safety placed me in a one on one position with people every single day. In addition, there was a job requirement to speak to large groups on a frequent basis. God was simply enlarging my mission field.

As a supervisor, a primary responsibility was preservation of the company's greatest resource, the employees. ***Human life was important and so was the salvation of the soul.*** Unfortunately, there were far too many accident investigations including fatality investigations.

However, my role of dealing with families and their loss was providential. There were obviously more than a few similarities between these two vocations. Jokingly, the phrase "safety during the week and salvation on the weekend" seemed appropriate. God truly had a plan and was controlling each step.

This secular vocation provided valuable experience in dealing with adversarial situations on several occasions. In one case, the facility manager urged a turn your head response to a deadly safety situation because of its potential adverse effect on production. Taking a firm stand your ground approach and affirming my belief that human life is more important than production did not set well with this manager. He threatened to jeopardize my retirement that was only a few months away. It was a rock and a hard place situation. But, having no doubt what God would want done, retirement or not, the value of human life confirmed my decision. After the dust settled, the company vice president called and applauded the decision. ***Doing the right thing always pays off.*** "Every Soul Matters".

Ironically, during these years, my wife and I started a ceramic shop next to our home just as a hobby. Working with clay and seeing the unfinished product, reminded us that we were just a work in progress. Much of our work ended up in the trash can. We just grew tired of trying to correct the flaws. Praise God, He never gives up on us, flaws and all.

God never throws us away even when we seem unusable. He just puts us on the shelf for a time until He is ready to put us back on His potter's wheel and, thru much pounding and shaping, tries to mold us again to the point we are usable.

Timing is Everything

There is no place in the Bible with a formula for balancing family, work, and ministry. And, if you add another dimension, such as school, just keeping up can be very frustrating. However, the Bible does have a formula for balancing our priorities.

It does emphasize an order of importance when it comes to family and ministry.

1Tim.3:4-5 "The minister is to manage his household well, with all dignity, keeping his children submissive, for if someone does not know how to manage his own household, how will he care for God's Church?" NKJV

Experience is a good teacher. Some basic principles apply for all the vocations to intertwine. First, the secular vocation chosen must not contradict the ministry.

One huge mistake by bivocational pastors is their choice of a secular career field that is not in line with biblical principles. For example, their chosen secular enterprise may be guilty of unethical business practices that results in a bad reputation that forces them to operate under dual values, one for their ministry and an entirely separate set for the other. In addition, their secular vocational choice could be so demanding that it leaves little time for ministry.

Second, the pastor must have the ability to identify priorities and balance his time between two careers.

Matthew 6:33 "But seek ye first the kingdom of God, and his righteousness; and all these things shall be added unto you." NKJV

Ministry effectiveness requires sound, Bible based, priority judgment. Which tasks should come first ahead of all the rest? A decision to do one thing automatically means that many other things must remain undone, and such decisions require that the person determines priorities in their life. Only by deciding what will have priority at a given time can a bivocational minister choose how to invest his time. Remember, God and His will always come first.

Genuine & Meaningful Influence

Our first son was a providential gift from God. With zero experience in child raising, we were just practicing parents with a lot to learn. Our son taught patience, unconditional love, and how to enjoy the insignificant things in life. I cannot underestimate the role he played in those early ministry years and continues to play to this day. Now, he is a grandfather himself and is a joy to watch as he deals with his own children and grandchildren. Life seems to have gone full circle for us.

The people dealt with at the steel mill introduced me to the first truly mean-spirited people that God would place in my path. More than a few folks along my path were not team players. One particular shift leader was a challenge. He taught lessons in forgiveness on more than one occasion. Fortunately, there were several good Christian people along the way. They made the work environment tolerable.

One of my early bosses was a bit testy. When I questioned his decisions, he would constantly respond with the phrase, - "life is not fair". God was teaching me how to deal with challenging and high maintenance people. It was difficult to maintain a testimony in an environment that was, at times, very hostile.

NO NEVER ALONE, NO NEVER ALONE;
HE PROMISED NEVER TO LEAVE ME,
NEVER TO LEAVE ME A LONE. unknown

SECTION II - SEARCHING BUT UNSETTLED

◆◆◆

SOUL SEARCHING

Looking Within

After more than ten years as a youth leader, God opened yet another providential door. God does work in mysterious ways. My wife and I went through a season in our late thirties and early forties when we both longed for a closer relationship with God. It was a mutual opinion that a different church environment would help.

Our family had grown with addition of another son. We had a growing concern for the spiritual welfare of the entire family. In hindsight, the stalemate in spiritual growth was more likely internal than external. However, the move proved to be providential. It was God's way of moving us to the next ministry opportunity. When God says go, the best response is to follow orders.

We started attending a small church just a few miles from home. Some close friends were also attending. We spent the time the first few years just sitting and soaking, but not getting involved. New young adults and young families began joining the church in increasing numbers. The demographics of the congregation was changing rapidly.

One of the young college age adults approached us after a Sunday service and asked if we would pray about leading a new Sunday School class to include all the young adults. Most of the young adults were attending the older adult classes and could not relate to the curriculum. We sensed the need and accepted the call.

There were fourteen students in attendance that first Sunday. The excitement level was over the top. The growth was so rapid, the class moved to the fellowship hall. To say that God blessed the ministry would be an understatement. The caring attitude among class members was unbelievable and a huge key to growth, both physically and spiritually.

It was during this time that my wife's father developed cancer of the mesentery. For ten months, we made a four-hour trip, on a weekly basis, to visit with him at a large cancer care facility. We cannot underestimate the prayers and support of this young adult class during this time. They sensed the need and answered the call. It was reciprocal.

Also, during this ministry phase, our youngest son answered the call to enter the gospel ministry. While only a young teen, he sensed the need and answered the call. God had obviously gifted him to preach and to serve early in his life and he responded. He continues to serve in ministry as he senses the need. His genuine excitement and enthusiasm for ministry had an insightful effect on my own decision to later answer the call. We had the blessed privilege of serving together on several occasions.

In the early nineties, my secular vocation began to take a new and exciting turn. After much earnest prayer, God opened a new door within my current work environment at the steel mill. The prayer was for a vocation where I could better serve people. God had placed the desire in my heart to become a more caring person even at this difficult workplace.

God, providentially, revealed a need within the workplace safety arena. He also made a way for my return to college. With the help, support, and patience of wife and family, I obtained a much-needed degree in safety.

The door of ministry opportunity that God had opened was quite remarkable. Steel company executives recognized my desire to serve in the safety field and offered the position of plant Safety Director. Now my ministry opportunity of caring for people had expanded 1000-fold. Sensing a need, I answered the call.

PRAY, PRAY, PRAY

God does answer prayer. He promised that, when we ask for things that are in line with His will for our lives, He will give us what we ask for.

1 John 5:14-15 "Now this is the confidence that we have in Him, that if we ask anything according to His will, He hears us. And if we know that He hears us, whatever we ask, we know that we have the petitions that we have asked of Him." NKJV

However, we may not always like His answer. God listens to all our prayers, regardless of how self-centered some may be.

Matthew 7:7 "Ask, and it will be given to you; seek, and you will find; knock, and it will be opened to you." NKJV

His answer may be "yes" or "no" or "not now." All our prayers should focus on things that honor and glorify God and reflect what the Bible clearly teaches. God's wisdom exceeds our own, and we absolutely must trust that His answers to our prayers are the best for us.

God wants the best for us. He does not want us to suffer without reason.

Psalm 46:10 "Be still and know that I am God; I will be exalted among the nations, I will be exalted in the earth!" NKJV

Living a life that is genuine and meaningful must be a life bathed in constant prayer never saying amen until the end of the day. Authentic spirit filled prayer results in an authentic ministry.

God Uses Unexpected People in Unusual Ways

During this period of ministry, God placed a person in my life that was a major factor in my journey. This gentleman was a high-ranking executive officer of the steel mill where I was serving as Safety Director. He was not a professing Christian. However, his love for people surfaced in his decision making. He was a good man. Our views on Christianity differed 180 degrees. However, respect was mutual. Many of future secular job decisions were based on his advice. Obviously, God uses people of different beliefs for our good and for His glory. To this day, prayers continue for his spiritual condition, but good people are often the most difficult to reach with the gospel message.

MAKE JESUS YOUR LIFE'S GUARD

A LATE IN LIFE CALL

Closing the Gap

As time raced on toward those inevitable middle-aged years, God was moving me spiritually as well. Retirement age finally arrived, at least, at the steel mill. At the early age of fifty-two, it was time to embark on another career. We never know what a day is going to bring, much less tomorrow and beyond.

It was during these years, that I experienced the most anointed call to date in this journey. Our church was conducting revival services that included two speakers each evening. While sitting on the back pew and intently listening to the first speaker, an elderly gentleman sat down next to me. Trying to be caring and helpful, I helped him find the speaker's text in his Bible. After the first speaker finished, the moderator began to introduce the second speaker. The speaker's name was a legendary name within our denomination. He was also a well-known evangelist. The older gentleman next to me rose to his feet. You guessed it, the next speaker turned and smiled at me, then took his place in the pulpit.

This old gentleman preached a strong and powerful sermon on answering the call. At the invitation, his plea included the statement “maybe there is someone here not so young anymore that God is calling into the gospel ministry”. God didn't need a ball bat to get my attention. That night, I sensed the need and answered God’s call to enter the gospel ministry.

However, I made the choice to remain bivocational. One reason, our area churches were not financially able to support full-time ministers. Even more importantly, I believed going outside the church walls afforded greater opportunities for ministry.

The next vocational opportunity came just ten days after my first retirement. The department chair in the Safety Technology Department at a local university called concerning an Assistant Professor position that had opened at the school. After an interview, I contracted to teach undergraduate and graduate classes within the workplace safety discipline. The opportunities to share my faith to a generation that was searching for truth abounded.

The theme in God's handiwork was becoming more obvious. It was no longer a question of balancing all my newfound responsibility, ***it was more a question of how to use each opportunity to evangelize and serve.*** His message was clear: look for the need wherever you are;whatever you are doing and answer the call.

It was during this time my wife's brother was experiencing kidney failure and had already lost the use of one kidney. My wife was a match and made the decision to donate her kidney. The blessings of that decision and ensuing journey were remarkable. At the top of the blessing list was her brother's decision to accept Christ.

During this time of trial and testing our church family came alongside to pray and to support. We cared for each other; we were family.

These were growing years, as well as a time of testing. It was a time of spiritual growth. God was teaching patience. There's an old song that reads "little is much when God is in it, labor not for wealth or fame, there's a soul and you can win it, if you'll go in Jesus' name." [3]

The gap was closing, God was making preparation for our ministry to older adults.

Made in God's Image

Spiritual growth is a process. It's a process of becoming more like Christ. When we trust Christ as Savior, the Holy Spirit begins the process. He wants us to conform to His image. 2 Peter 1:3-8 reflects God's plan.

"As His divine power has given to us all things that pertain to life and godliness, through the knowledge of Him who called us by glory and virtue, by which have been given to us exceedingly great and precious promises, that through these you may be partakers of the divine nature, having escaped the corruption that is in the world through lust. But also, for this very reason, giving all diligence, add to your faith virtue, to virtue knowledge, to knowledge self-control, to self-control perseverance, to perseverance godliness, to godliness brotherly kindness, and to brotherly kindness love. For if these things are yours and abound, you will be neither barren nor unfruitful in the knowledge of our Lord Jesus Christ." NKJV

So, by the power of God, we have everything we need to live Godly lives. That is the goal of spiritual growth. Notice, what we need comes through our knowledge of Him, which is the key to obtaining everything we need.

When the miracle of salvation occurs, spiritual growth begins.

The Holy Spirit indwells us.

John 14:16 "And I will pray the Father, and He will give you another Helper, that He may abide with you forever." NKJV

We are made new in Christ.

2 Corinthians 5:17 "Therefore, if anyone is in Christ, he is a new creation; old things have passed away; behold, all things have become new." NKJV

The natural man starts to yield to the new man. Spiritual growth is an ongoing and daily process that takes a lifetime. The success of spiritual growth depends on our study and practical application of His Word. Prayer and spiritual growth go hand in hand.

Ask God for biblical wisdom and spiritual growth follows. Ask God for opportunities to serve and spiritual growth follows. Ask God to help you overcome sin and spiritual growth follows. Ask God to make you more genuine as a Christian and spiritual growth will follow. Ask God to add purpose and meaning to your life and spiritual growth follows.

God is Always on Time

The old preacher that just showed up during the revival service, tops the list as most influential in my decision to answer God's call to the gospel ministry. He was a genuine, humble, God anointed instrument of change in my life. I am convinced that God sent him to speak a special message, at a special time, at a special church to a not so special person. I knew, in my heart, that God was working prior to this day, but his God sent message put me over the top. I have never doubted that decision even during the days of trial and tribulation that would occur only a few years later.

THIS LITTLE LIGHT OF MINE

IN THE INTERIM

Pastors Come & Go

Soon after answering God's call to the gospel ministry, the pastor of our church asked me to serve as Associate Pastor. He graciously provided me many opportunities to preach. Our church was building a new sanctuary at the time. I thoroughly enjoyed our ministry together. The church was growing rapidly.

Pulpit supply opportunities in surrounding churches were numerous. On one occasion, I wrecked my truck on an icy bridge going for coffee prior to one such appointment. I suffered a mild concussion as a result. I believe that God wanted to convey a message to me early on: ***"the gospel ministry is to be taken seriously; it is a matter with eternal importance".*** He got my attention.

Suddenly, our Senior Pastor resigned to accept a call at another church. ***Sometimes, God slows physical church growth to facilitate more spiritual growth.*** I suddenly found myself thrust into the position as Interim Pastor, a position held until the pulpit committee selected the next Senior Pastor.

God had supplied just a taste and the experience of pastoring a church. However, I'm afraid my inexperience manifested itself in my performance. Thankfully, most people were gracious. From that time forward, it became clear that God does not allow his servants to just sit and soak. More interim pastor opportunities began to open.

The next call would come from a church in our old hometown. I agreed to fill the position for six months or until another senior pastor was located. God was developing a deep personal passion for the interim pastor ministry. The position required preaching the gospel plus loving and caring for the people. It was obvious that this was God's call on my life. My wife felt the same way and shared the same passion for the people.

The hardest part of the interim ministry is leaving. Falling in love with the people just happens and your spiritual family enlarges with each ministry call.

During these interim ministry years, I was able to retire from teaching at the local university. To fill the gap, a safety consulting business opportunity developed. The business grew and eventually employed the entire family. My wife and I both became officers in the business. This business would prove to be a key factor in providing future ministry opportunities. Needs materialized that we were unaware of previously. The variety of business ventures introduced us to a totally different group of demographics. We met people from all walks of life. There was a chance to make a genuine and meaningful difference in people's lives. Every task and group of people were different.

The business engaged in everything from safety consulting, demolition, hazardous waste materials cleanup, to private investigation and security. The fields were truly white and ready to harvest. The interim pastor ministry was a perfect fit.

Soon, an interim call came in from a church in another state just a few miles from home. However, it was a longer commute than the earlier interim calls. Fire had destroyed the church building and the congregation was meeting in a nearby school. On top of that, the preacher had just resigned. After much prayer, God gave a sense of peace about the call. The church could only afford to supply expense money, but that was acceptable. My ministry goal was to restore hope and bring unity. My wife and youngest son joined me in this endeavor. The interim lasted for a year. Soon after the new church building project completed, we said goodbye. It was a bittersweet time in our ministry.

The next interim opportunity provided the first experience working with senior adults. A nearby church asked that I serve as their Interim Senior Adult Pastor. We both fell in love with this group of seniors. It was one of the most pleasant and joy filled experiences to date. It was an absolute joy to serve with this Senior Pastor. His mentoring skills helped keep situations and people in perspective. After a year we would say our roughest goodbye to this church and group of super seniors.

Lead Others and Follow God

According to the Bible, working with a local congregation, serving its many needs, and helping it set up various ministries are all gifts of leadership.

Romans 12:8 "He who exhorts, in exhortation; he who gives, with liberality; he who leads, with diligence; he who shows mercy, with cheerfulness." NKJV

The Greek word for rule used in many verses means one who is placed over others.

1 Thessalonians 5:12 "And we beseech you, brethren, to know them which labor among you and are over (rule) you in the Lord." NKJV

The more gifted the leadership, the better the group functions. A group's potential is often a measure of effective leadership. It's the same in the secular world.

Leaders are to constantly watch their flock and be willing to sacrifice to rescue the sheep. Spiritual leaders should possess the ability to recognize that their leadership position is God given and under His control. They understand that they don't drive the flock from the rear but lead by example from the front. They are constantly emphasizing that Christ is the Head of the Church.

A truly God appointed Christian leader understands that he is only a slave of Christ and serves those he leads.

James, the half-brother of Jesus, had the gift of leadership as he led the church in Jerusalem. He referred to himself as "a servant of God and of the Lord Jesus Christ". James had the ability to encourage biblical thinking among his peers. James dealt with very contentious issues but was very persuasive in his arguments. He was a God gifted leader.

Gifted leaders use due diligence and discernment. These leaders pass on these traits to people they lead. ***Spiritual leadership offers a tremendous level of purpose to those that answer the call.*** However, to those who are less than genuine or misinterpret the call, the results can be destructive both to the individual and the church.

Looking Back at Providence

The gentleman that called and offered the first official interim in my old hometown was also one of the elders in the church where I grew up. He and his congregation were so encouraging and kind. The church was an old historic building, but the spirit of the people was warm and refreshing. This wonderful experience added to the conviction that my decision to serve in the interim ministry position in churches without, or in between, pastors was a God anointed decision.

The out of state calling was from one of my former workmates at the steel mill. Many of the members of this church were steel mill retirees. Being involved in their building program provided experience that would prove to be useful in later years at a church many miles from home. God does work in mysterious ways. Little did I realize, when working at the mill with these men, that we would someday serve together in ministry. The year at this location was a year well spent.

By far, the most positive and encouraging experience during this period of ministry was my interim as Senior Adult Pastor. The pastor was one of the most loving and Godly men that I had the privilege of serving with to date. His mentoring helped prepare me for the trial and practical ministry education that lay ahead. The senior adults at this church were some of the most spiritual people that I had met as well, a credit to this pastor's spiritual leadership.

SECTION III - HARD KNOCKS GRAD SCHOOL

STORMS ON THE HORIZON

ENTRANCE EXAM

The Destruction of Self-sufficiency

The next call came from a deacon at a nearby church that was currently without a pastor and the deacon's plea seemed one of desperation. I believe he had reached the bottom of the available preacher barrel. The deacon asked me to come and fill the pulpit on a certain Sunday. I cordially accepted and was excited with the opportunity. ***Preachers do love to preach.***

After a few more guest speaking engagements, I accepted an Interim Pastor position. The congregational vote total was 100%. All the members present affirmed the decision. I felt very honored. The salary was not great, but this was not about money. It was about sensing a need and answering a call.

The church was in a very culturally diverse area. Drug and alcohol problems near the church proved to be a deterrent and an unwelcome environment for potential new members. The church was typical of many city churches nation wide experiencing similar problems.

I had unknowingly entered the school of hard knocks.

Having passed the entrance exam, I was about to experience a curriculum that would match the requirements of the most challenging theological seminary.

After a few months, the deacons approached and offered a full-time Senior Pastor position. There was no salary increase in the package. God was teaching humbleness. I went against personal policy, colleague's advice, and gut feeling and accepted the offer. The decision was also contrary to my personal interim pastor rules.

I'm reminded now that Jacob of Old Testament time also made many bad decisions, but God still blessed him. Despite of my ill-advised decision, God blessed the ministry in a mighty way. Many accepted Christ, rededications were frequent, and church growth was phenomenal. Numbers had quadrupled in a brief time even at the midweek services.

There were many opportunities to both cry and laugh. The church had many saints go on to glory and we celebrated their homegoing. On a humorous note, one of the members decided to use a new funeral service in town. It was a memorable occasion in so many ways. The funeral director had neglected to put fuel in the hearse prior to the service. Too add insult to injury, the driver's side door would not open. And since the funeral time was late in the afternoon, the graveside part of the service concluded the day under lights - car headlights.

The church family was pitching in and helping to serve. Thank God for family. They had a genuine heart for the Lord. They were united in cause and purpose.

The experience also taught me that the best, and most biblical way, to deal with an occasional disagreement was to love everyone unconditionally in every situation.

Remember, "every soul matters".

It Came to Pass, Not to Stay

Recognize first and foremost that testing comes from God. When God tests us, He does us a great service. In both Testaments, the word used for test means to prove by trial. The purpose of God's testing is to examine our faith. God does not need to prove it to Himself, but He wants to prove to us that our faith is genuine and that we are really His children.

In the Bible, Jesus uses the Parable of the Sower, to illustrate His purpose. He identifies those who fall away as the people who receive the seed of God's Word with joy, but as soon as the test comes, they drift away. According to James, ***the testing of our faith develops perseverance, which leads to Christian maturity.*** James also says that testing is a blessing, because, when it's all over and we have passed the test, we will receive the prize.

James 1:12 "Blessed is the man who endures temptation; for when he has been approved, he will receive the crown of life which the Lord has promised to those who love Him." NKJV

The tests we endure come in a variety of ways. Becoming an active serving Christian will often require us to come out of our comfort zones. But, staying the course during the testing results in spiritual growth.

James 1:2 "Consider it pure joy, my brothers, whenever you face trials of many kinds." NKJV

Testing comes in insignificant ways such as minor irritations or they may be severe in nature. Regardless of the size of the test, we benefit from the trial.

Job is a good example of how God's allows Satan to test

the saints. Yet, Job did not sin.

Job 1:22 "In all this Job did not sin nor charge God with wrong." NKJV

Job's ordeal proves that no demon can test beyond what God allows. Without testing, we can never find or achieve our God planned purpose. Testing is a positive spiritual growth essential.

Experiencing trials in life yields strength like a mighty oak tree that digs its roots deeper to increase its staying power. ***Dig your roots deep into His Word and grip His promises, so you can survive every storm that comes your way.***

For a certainty, God will never allow testing beyond what we are able to endure. Paul said to the Corinthians:

2 Cor. 12:10 "Therefore I take pleasure in infirmities, in reproaches, in needs, in persecutions, in distresses, for Christ's sake. For when I am weak, then I am strong." NKJV

Meaningful on the Job Training

The influencers at this church were too many to mention. However, there were a few standouts. One lady was a very spirit filled individual with a constant positive and encouraging attitude. However, to counter that, a few were in opposition to my ministry methods and ways.

On one occasion, the Spirit moved one precious senior saint to shout and take a lap around the church. A mentally challenged young man would occasionally start waving his arms and hands in agreement with the message. Still others would loudly amen or shout their praises. God was strengthening my spirit of compassion even toward those that occassionally opposed the work.

When peace, like a river, attendeth my way,
When sorrows like sea billows roll;
Whatever my lot, thou hast taught me to say,
It is well, it is well with my soul. [10]

TOUGH FINALS

I Peter 5:8 "Be sober, be vigilant; because your adversary the devil walks about like a roaring lion, seeking whom he may devour." NKJV

No Christian servant who is trying to follow God's will escapes trials and troubles. It just goes with the territory.

John 16:33 "These things I have spoken to you, that in Me you may have peace. In the world you will have tribulation; but be of good cheer, I have overcome the world." NKJV

People were joining the church with such frequency that proper screening and discipling seemed impossible. In hindsight, I should have taken the time. The grade on that exam was less than passing.

A small group of members held the opinion that too much church growth was not a good thing. There seemed to be a fear of losing that close family worship environment that small churches enjoy. I understood and respected their opinion.

However, satan was very much real and despised what God was doing at this church. His method was to divide and conquer. He was using differing opinions to sow seeds of discord.

No one should have been surprised at the power of evil. Satan and his forces had driven a wedge between a few good people. The small group of people in opposition to the work were not bad people. Most of the members at the church were extremely supportive of our ministry. However, a small minority did not agree with our ministry goals. ***I realized that compassion cannot be limited to those who agree with your position or methods.*** Compassion knows no boundaries. We loved all of these people even the dissenters.

God had allowed an experience with more challenging situations than any theological degree would have provided. God had allowed the experience with every type of personality imaginable from the sweet and congenial to very gruff and difficult. Graduation from this school of hard knocks was getting near.

2 Tim. 4:7 "I have run the race, kept the faith, and finished the course." NKJV

After four wonderful years with these folks, it was time to move on, better said, graduate. Contributing to this decision to move on was a health scare. Trying to run a business, pastor a church, and keep up with family demands had taken their toll on my health. Ending up in the hospital emergency room with a possible heart attack was an attention getter. Praise God, it was more of an anxiety attack. It was obvious that God was, providentially, moving us onward and upward.

Disrupted and Disturbed

James 3 references good and evil and the inevitable outcome of each.

James 3:13-18 "Who is wise and understanding among you? Let him show by good conduct that his works are done in the meekness of wisdom. But if you have bitter envy and self-seeking in your hearts, do not boast and lie against the truth. This wisdom does not descend from above, but is earthly, sensual, demonic. For where envy and self-seeking exist, confusion and every evil thing are there. But the wisdom that is from above is first pure, then peaceable, gentle, willing to yield, full of mercy and good fruits, without partiality and without hypocrisy. Now the fruit of righteousness is sown in peace by those who make peace." NKJV

Self-seeking agenda can destroy a God movement faster than a rotten potato can destroy the whole bag. Disunity that results in church splits are sad and discouraging events that, unfortunately, occur in the Lord's church. The results of a church split can be both destructive and demoralizing.

Churches are like medical facilities, full of the sick and the wounded. However, with the church the sickness is often sin and the wounds are often those members inflict on each other. No member is perfect, and no leader is perfect including the pastor. With imperfect people sometimes comes misunderstanding and disagreements. The favorite song unfortunately becomes: "I'll have my own way Lord, I'll have my own way, I am the potter and you are the clay".

We react to situations by picking sides and wagging our tongues. As a result, the split worsens, and more families and even neighbors feel the effect. Splits occur when someone tries to orchestrate situations to meet their own agenda. Quite often it's about power. Someone wants to take leadership away from the pastor and gathers a group of followers to carry out his or her purpose. Unfortunately, music and worship style opinion are too often cause of disunity.

Excuses for the conflict abound. However, they all have the same root - pride and self-centeredness.

James 4:1-3 "where do wars and fights come from among you? Do they not come from your desires for pleasure that war in your members? You lust and do not have. You murder and covet and cannot obtain. You fight and war. Yet you do not have because you do not ask. You ask and do not receive, because you ask amiss, that you may spend it on your pleasures." NKJV

To add to the problem, tragically many members in today's churches are not truly born again.

Matthew 7:16-23 "You will know them by their fruits. Do men gather grapes from thorn bushes or figs from thistles? Even so, every good tree bears good fruit, but a bad tree bears bad fruit. A good tree cannot bear bad fruit, nor can a bad tree bear good fruit. Every tree that does not bear good fruit is cut down and thrown into the fire. Therefore, by their fruits you will know them. Not everyone who says to Me, 'Lord, Lord,' shall enter the kingdom of heaven, but he who does the will of My Father in heaven. Many will say to Me in that day, 'Lord, Lord, have we not prophesied in Your name, cast out demons in Your name, and done many wonders in Your name?' And then I will declare to them, 'I never knew you; depart from Me, you who practice lawlessness!' NKJV

The exercise of prudence, wisdom and even disciplines may be necessary.

Matthew 18:15-20 "Moreover if your brother sins against you, go and tell him his fault between you and him alone. If he hears you, you have gained your brother. But if he will not hear, take with you one or two more, that 'by the mouth of two or three witnesses every word may be established.' And if he refuses to hear them, tell it to the church. But if he refuses even to hear the church, let him be to you like a heathen and a tax collector. Assuredly, I say to you, whatever you bind on earth will be bound in heaven, and whatever you lose on earth will be loosed in heaven. Again, I say to you that if two of you agree on earth concerning anything that they ask, it will be done for them by My Father in heaven. For where two or three are gathered together in My name, I am there in the midst of them." NKJV

The daily exposure of church members to hours of immorality, compared to only to an hour of church is a huge part of the problem. ***Our liberal culture influences church members so much that they begin to mimic that behavior.*** The world's agenda is all about self-promotion. The world's agenda results in dissension, jealousy and strife. When this agenda works its way into the church, there will be trouble.

Titus 2:11-13 contains the solution.

"For the grace of God that brings salvation has appeared to all men, teaching us that, denying ungodliness and worldly lusts, we should live soberly, righteously, and godly in the present age, looking for the blessed hope and glorious appearing of our great God and Savior Jesus Christ." NKJV

God's Word has the answers to all of life's problems.

Philippians 2:3 "Let nothing be done through selfish ambition or conceit, but in lowliness of mind let each esteem others better than himself." NKJV

Humility coupled with repentance heals church disunity. Accepting each other's apology followed by the display of Christian love results in victory for Christ and the church.

Genuine People Have Nothing to Hide

The causes of problems in the church are many. The fact that Jesus Christ is removed from the throne and self-serving interest takes His place is the main reason for church issues, minor or major. If each member in the church is set on doing God's will and on Christ honoring worship, there may still be minor differences of opinion, but the differences are settled in a loving and Godlike manner.

POST-GRADUATION

Your Troubles and Trials Will Soon be Over

When God wants to drill a man, and thrill a man, and skill a man; When God wants to mold a man to play the noblest part; When He yearns with all His heart to create so great and bold a man that all the world shall be amazed, watch His methods, watch His ways!
How He ruthlessly perfects whom He royally elects!
How He hammers him and hurts him and with mighty blows converts him into trial shapes of clay which only God understands; while his tortured heart is crying, and he lifts beseeching hands! How He bends but never breaks when his good He undertakes; How He uses whom He chooses and with every purpose fuses him; by every act induces him to try His splendor out, God knows what He's about. Author Unknown

God had made it obvious that it was time for us to move on. Confirmation of the decision to retire would soon come in a series of amazing events.

Our human decision, or so we thought, was to close the business, retire from the ministry, sell our home and move to Florida. My sister and brother-in-law lived in Florida and we discovered, through frequent vacations, that the environment was very inviting. We had no idea that God agreed, at least partly, and was orchestrating the way.

The consulting business did close through a series of miraculous events, but my proposed retirement from the ministry was not final as we were to discover later. Our house sold in three days to a lady with cash at the full asking price. We packed up, put our furniture in storage, and left for Florida with no forwarding address. We were simply trusting God to do the rest.

God is indeed a God of miracles. My sister and brother-in-law were staying at their far north summer home and encouraged us to use their Florida home until we could find our own place. We eventually chose a fifth-floor condominium near the ocean with a one-year lease until we could settle on a more permanent abode. Step-by-step God does lead his dear children along.

The decision concerning church attendance was a bit more difficult. We had been through a period of intense on the job training and we were going to take our time with that decision. For now, we would attend my sister and brother-in-law's church and, before long, started attending their LifeGroup. We wanted nothing to do with a ministry. We were just going to sit and soak. I was retired.

This recess in our ministry proved to be a time of soul-searching and spiritual growth. God was preparing us for something far beyond our imagination.

While working in the safety field at the mill, there were many locked doors with warning signs such as "Danger High Voltage, Qualified Personnel Only". What did that sign mean? In short, if you know little or nothing about electricity, stay out. Disobeying the sign could have been fatal. Contact with high voltage kills. To enter that door would have been foolish.

The experience gained from my last pastorate was an absolute necessity, but it did leave us asking; God, why did you close that door?

Brokenness and Closed Doors

When God closes a door, as in our experience, a lot of soul searching and time alone with God is necessary. Numerous biblical examples offer good reason for spending time alone.

Moses met with God alone at the burning bush experience and again on Mt. Sinai. David in his Psalms spoke of a time alone with God. God's presence passed by as Elijah was in the cave.

Matthew 6:6 commands us to spend quiet time with God.

"But you, when you pray, go into your room, and when you have shut your door, pray to your Father who is in the secret place; and your Father who sees in secret will reward you openly." NKJV

Proverbs 3:5-6 tells us "Trust in the Lord with all your heart and lean not on your own understanding; In all your ways acknowledge Him, And He shall direct your paths." NKJV

When God closes a door, he closes it for a good purpose. Closed doors take many forms. It could be a business opportunity, a ministry opportunity, or a new vocational venture. However, when God closes that door, it is because He loves us and wants the best for us. He wants to protect and lead us. The Lord is our Shepherd leading us to green pastures and still waters.

It is so easy to fall for the old human natural man trap of thinking that we know what's best for us. We may have the best of lofty intentions, but to pry open, or reopen a closed door could be disastrous. Always trust that God knows what is best for our present and our future. Remember, God loves us and only wants to keep us on the straight and narrow.

Pain and suffering fill our world. One of the most asked and tough questions in ministry work is "Why do bad things happen to good people?". Let's consider some known biblical facts: First, we serve a sovereign God, so everything that happens, He, at least, allows. Secondly, ***we are only human, and we should never expect to understand an omniscient, omnipotent, omnipresent God.***

Consider the righteous man, named Job.

Job 1:1 "There was a man in the land of Uz, whose name was Job; and that man was blameless and upright, and one who feared God and shunned evil." NKJV

However, Job suffered in unbelievable ways. God allowed Satan to do anything he wanted to Job, except take his life, and Satan met the challenge.

How did Job respond?

Job 13:15 "Though He slay me, yet will I trust Him. Even so, I will defend my own ways before Him" Job 1:21 "And he said: "Naked I came from my mother's womb, and naked shall I return there. The Lord gave, and the Lord has taken away; Blessed be the name of the Lord." NKJV

Did Job understand what God was doing - no. However, Job trusted God even in a tough situation. Lesson for us: Respond in the same manner. Just trust God.

We must acknowledge that there is no one good, no not one.

Romans 3:23 "For all have sinned and come short of the glory of God." NKJV

Jesus said in Luke 18:19 "Why do you call Me good? No one is good but One, that is, God." NKJV

Sin affects everyone either directly or indirectly. Sin can be personal, or sin can be corporate. Let's face it, our world has fallen, and the crushing effects of the fall are universal. That may seem unjust, but we have no right to question God.

Remember: Bad things do happen to good people, but this

world is not our final home.

2 Corinthians 4:16–18 "Therefore we do not lose heart. Even though our outward man is perishing, yet the inward man is being renewed day by day. For our light affliction, which is but for a moment, is working for us a far more exceeding and eternal weight of glory, while we do not look at the things which are seen, but at the things which are not seen. For the things which are seen are temporary, but the things which are not seen are eternal." NKJV

Heaven is our reward and it will be beyond our imagination.

Remember: Bad things do happen to good people, but God has a purpose for everything.

Romans 8:28 "And we know that all things work together for good to those who love God, to those who are the called according to His purpose." NKJV

Consider Joseph.

Genesis 50:19–21 "Joseph said to them, "Do not be afraid, for am I in the place of God? But as for you, you meant evil against me; but God meant it for good, to bring it about as it is this day, to save many people alive. Now therefore, do not be afraid; I will provide for you and your little ones." And he comforted them and spoke kindly to them." NKJV

Remember: Bad things do happen to good people, but God may be preparing us for a more intense ministry.

2 Corinthians 1:3–5 "Blessed be the God and Father of our Lord Jesus Christ, the Father of mercies and God of all comfort, who comforts us in all our tribulation, that we may be able to comfort those who are in any trouble, with the comfort with which we ourselves are comforted by God. For as the sufferings of Christ abound in us, so, our consolation also abounds through Christ." NKJV

Those with scars of war can better serve those going through the war.

Remember: Bad things do happen to good people, and God's absolute best may be in store for the worst.

1 Peter 2:20–23 "For what credit is it if, when you are beaten for your faults, you take it patiently? But when you do good and suffer, if you take it patiently, this is commendable before God. For to this you were called, because Christ also suffered for us, leaving us an example, that you should follow His steps: "Who committed no sin, Nor was deceit found in His mouth"; who, when He was reviled, did not revile in return; when He suffered, He did not threaten, but committed Himself to Him who judges righteously;" NKJV

Certainly, Jesus knew pain.

Romans 5:8 "But God demonstrates His own love toward us, in that while we were still sinners, Christ died for us." NKJV

How much did Jesus love us? He stretched out his arms and died for us.

Romans 6:23 "For the wages of sin is death, but the gift of God is eternal life in Christ Jesus our Lord." NKJV

When we belong to Jesus, everything happens for a reason. Jesus Christ our Lord and Savior never wastes a hurt. Know this and let it soak in, God is good, God is just, God is loving, and God is merciful.

Psalm 135:3 "Praise the Lord, for the Lord is good; Sing praises to His name, for it is pleasant." NKJV

When bad things do happen, never doubt His goodness, just trust Him. God often uses brokenness, at times in the form of closed doors, to better prepare us for the next open door. Brokenness in the life of the believer is an absolute must for spiritual growth. ***The just shall walk by faith and not by sight.***

Genuine & Meaningful Quiet Moments

This period was a lonely, dry, desert like experience in our ministry journey. Since, it was a time for quiet reflection, we limited our interaction with others. It was just the two of us and God.

We spent time enjoying God's creation during our beach walks and bike rides. The sun coming up over the beautiful Atlantic constantly reminded us that God is still God. We knew everything would be okay in God's time and in God's way.

There were certainly no complaints about our lodging place and location. God does take care of His own. We were under His wings and we felt very blessed.

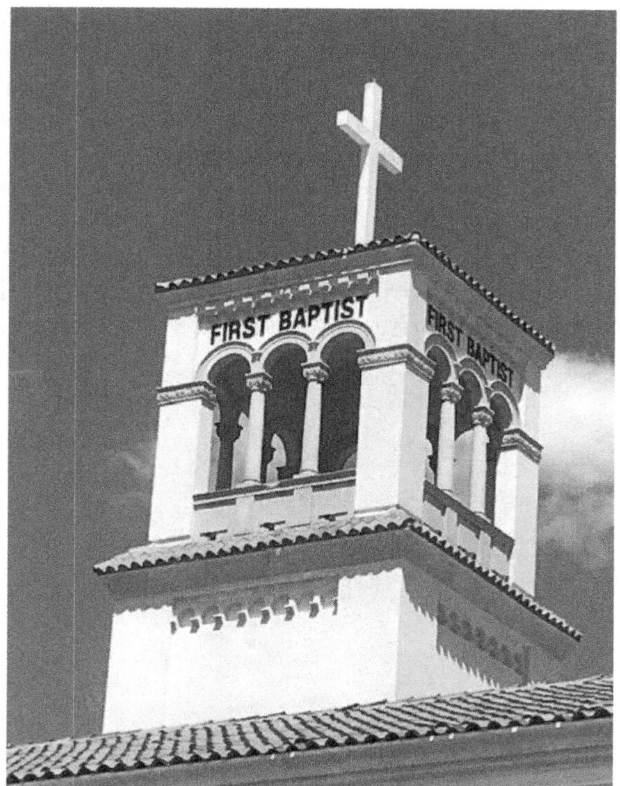

A CHANGE OF SCENERY

PART TWO - AN ANOINTED VOYAGE

The Anointing

In biblical times, lice and the like were deadly to sheep. Their infestation into the wool and the sheep's ears quite often was fatal. So, oil was an effective solution. The wool became too slick for insects to land on. Therefore, anointing became a symbol of protection and the giving of supernatural power.

One Biblical Greek word for anoint is 'chrio', which means to coat with oil. In theology, the word anoint means to sanctify for service. Some Biblical examples of spiritual anointing appear in several Old Testament passages.

Exodus 29:7 "And you shall take the anointing oil, pour it on his head and anoint him." NKJV

Exodus 40:9 "And you shall take the anointing oil and anoint the tabernacle and all that is in it; and you shall hallow it and all its utensils, and it shall be holy." NKJV

2 Kings 9:6 "Then he arose and went into the house. And he poured the oil on his head, and said to him, "Thus says the Lord God of Israel: 'I have anointed you king over the people of the Lord, over Israel." NKJV

Ecclesiastes 9:8 "Let your garments always be white and let your head lack no oil." NKJV

James 5:14 "Is anyone among you sick? Let him call for the elders of the church, and let them pray over him, anointing him with oil in the name of the Lord." NKJV

The oil has no power and is only symbolic. It symbolizes the providential direction and application of His power on a person's life. A good application could be someone picked out or chosen to perform a specific task at a specific time and in a specific location. Again, scripture contains some notable examples.

Luke 4:18-19 'The Spirit of the Lord is upon Me, Because He has anointed Me To preach the gospel to the poor; He has sent Me to heal the brokenhearted, to proclaim liberty to the captives and recovery of sight to the blind, to set at liberty those who are oppressed. To proclaim the acceptable year of the Lord." NKJV

Acts 10:38 "How God anointed Jesus of Nazareth with the Holy Spirit and with power, who went about doing good and healing all who were oppressed by the devil, for God was with Him." NKJV

John 14:16 And I will pray the Father, and He will give you another Helper, that He may abide with you forever.

Anointing Does Apply to Every Christian.

1 John 2:20 "But you have an anointing from the Holy One, and you know all things." NKJV

2 Corinthians 1:21-22 "Now He who establishes us with you in Christ and has anointed us is God, who also has sealed us and given us the Spirit in our hearts as a guarantee." NKJV

SECTION I - LIGHTHOUSE MOMENTS

FOGGY DAYS

Then One Day in a Quiet Place

Time alone with God would soon yield results. Despite the attempts to enjoy the full benefits of retirement, secular vocational opportunities continued to develop. It seemed God was forcing a decision between a secular vocation, versus a more committed involvement in a ministry of sorts.

The secular vocation required a great deal of travel. Many of the safety consulting assignments required travel three to five days a week. However, I used these opportunities to subtly proclaim the gospel, and even incorporate the gospel message into the safety training agenda. I never received a complaint from either client or employer. In fact, and refreshing as well, they encouraged my folksy preaching style of teaching safety.

There was never a need to cloak my strong belief in Christ behind a more professional business-like approach. The experience, even though secular in title, was very spiritual in nature. God paved the way, removed every roadblock, and turned each consulting assignment into a blessing.

Eventually, after prayerfully finding and moving into a more permanent Florida home, consulting opportunities began to decline. Providentially, at the same time the encouragement for more ministry involvement from some loving members of our new church family increased. The response, at first, was straight from the book: "I'll pray about it". The church was experiencing a season of testing at the time which added to the delay in my answer.

It is possible to delay answering God's call too long. Holy Spirit pressure can be intense and overwhelming. Perhaps, substituting LifeGroup teaching on infrequent occasions would satisfy those internal and external stirrings. That was my plan, but it wasn't God's plan or purpose. But thankfully, God is a patient God.

Once again, just as in my early pre-salvation years, two men had a profound influence on my future involvement in ministry. As before, both were genuine and both were men of purpose. One was retired pastor, the other an active deacon. The retired pastor was still actively serving in the church teaching ministry. Both were, unknowingly, actively serving in a ministry of mentoring and encouragement. Both have gone on to Glory, but their influence left its mark. In fact, as providence would dictate, it was my honor and privilege to take part in both homegoing services.

God used both genuine Godly men to move me into the deacon ministry. The blessings enjoyed and the lessons learned in this deacon ministry opportunity would prove priceless in later years. The ministry also supplied opportunity to become more personally involved in the lives of our new church family. God was blessing and He was also teaching and preparing.

Further heart softening and preparation came from my two-week mission trip to Brazil. Seeing the great hunger for the gospel among the Brazilian people and preaching in their churches and on street corners clearly affected my future ministry decisions.

Serving in a local inter-denominational church as an Associate Pastor for one year during this period also strengthened my desire to return to the pastorate. The encouragement from this experience was remarkable. Against the odds, a senior adult was saved and baptized. It was a memorable year well spent.

Eventually, the part-time adult LifeGroup teaching involvement became full-time. Retirement was truly over. Thank God that he allows new and fresh starts.

The Gift of Encouragement

There is an old saying that comes to mind: "Nobody likes me, everybody hates me, I think I'll go eat worms!" Unknown

Be honest, when is the last time you encouraged someone? When is the last time you said, "thank you for all you do for our Lord"? Just how important is the gift of encouragement?

Acts 4:36-37 "And Joses, who was also named Barnabas by the apostles (which is translated Son of Encouragement), a Levite of the country of Cyprus, having land, sold it, and brought the money and laid it at the apostles' feet." NKJV

Barnabas was an unsung hero. Encouragement reflected itself in his actions and his attitude. His example is so important, God's Word mentions him. Acts 11 and Acts 13 mentions Barnabas, but he is never in a position of prominence. He is simply an encourager.

Barnabas recognized his God given ability and encouraged others in ministry. He demonstrated no jealousy or hidden agenda, only encouragement. He even saw the positive traits of Mark later in Acts and encouraged Paul to give him another chance. Paul disagreed and went his own way.

Everyone needs a word of encouragement. The widow or widower, the single mom or dad, the struggling married couple, the downtrodden, the homeless, the discouraged pastor all need just a word of encouragement. Do you realize that ***just a word of encouragement may be the catalyst that moves someone to the next level in their spiritual experience?***

Find someone who fits the description and poor out your love and appreciation then watch God work. Never fail to give people another chance. That's what Jesus would do. Plenty of people in God's Word failed miserably, but after forgiveness and a little or a lot of encouragement, went on to become great in the Kingdom.

Genuine & Purposeful People

Without a doubt, God intervened to providentially change my semi-retirement plans into His purpose and for His glory. The response from me was optional. God does give us choices. The response would either be self-centered or God-centered. Through much prayer, and the influence of Godly people, the correct answer was never clearer.

However, the next chapter in my journey was about to take an unexpected route.

God does work in mysterious ways and at unexpected times to carry out His purpose in our lives. My personal choices would not have resulted in the same results. The need to allow God to lead is a learned lesson that comes from trying to swim against the current. ***When we throw up our hands, God does His greatest work.*** God wants us at the end of our rope so His Glory can shine.

An often-misunderstood verse is *1 Cor. 10:13*.

"No temptation has overtaken you except such as is common to man; but God is faithful, who will not allow you to be tempted beyond what you are able, but with the temptation will also make the way of escape, that you may be able to bear it." NKJV

This verse only applies to the temptation to sin. It has nothing to do with situations used by God to test and strengthen our faith and reliance on Him. Our Heavenly Father wants us to have more challenges than we can handle. Then, we must rely on Him.

A NEW PORT OF CALL

The Best was Yet to Come

E*phesian 4:11-13 "And He Himself gave some to be apostles, some prophets, some evangelists, and some pastors and teachers, for the equipping of the saints for the work of ministry, for the edifying of the body of Christ, till we all come to the unity of the faith and of the knowledge of the Son of God, to a perfect man, to the measure of the stature of the fullness of Christ."* NKJV

Overwhelmingly blessed with the opportunity to lead the senior adult LifeGroup, our close church family grew exponentially. The class was a mini church with music and fellowship included. In actuality, the numbers were greater in this group than in some of our earlier church ministry experiences.

What was God's purpose in introducing us to so many in our church family? The answer would eventually become abundantly clear. The LifeGroup directors, the deacons, the pastors, and the wonderful, beautiful people from all walks of life that poured out their unconditional acceptance and love in the good times and the tough times were, and continue to be, some of the crown jewels in our ministry journey. More of these precious jewels appeared later in the next phase of the journey. They were genuine people with a genuine love and a genuine purpose. Sadly, some of these precious people have gone home. That's another chapter entirely.

The church entered a transition period during this part of our race to Heaven's finish line. The Senior Pastor resigned, an Interim Pastor was elected, and a search committee selected. However, our LifeGroup continued week by week and, at times, day by day. A few left the church, but most stayed the course. This transitional period proved to be one of spiritual growth both individually and corporately. ***The time spent would prove to separate the genuine from the not so genuine, the true servants from the pew warmers, and the authentic from the inauthentic.***

Matthew 16:17-19 "Jesus answered and said to him, "Blessed are you, Simon Bar-Jonah, for flesh and blood has not revealed this to you, but My Father who is in heaven. And I also say to you that you are Peter, and on this rock, I will build My church, and the gates of Hades shall not prevail against it. And I will give you the keys of the kingdom of heaven, and whatever you bind on earth will be bound in heaven, and whatever you lose on earth will be loosed in heaven." NKJV

Just prior to this transitional period God was blessing the church spiritually but challenging the church financially. Some staff positions were abandoned out of necessity. However, even those tough decisions resulted in providential blessings to those involved. ***When God closes one door to the faithful, he always opens another.***

Concern over the loss of staff was voiced by several senior adults. There was a sense of abandonment. Sensing the need and remembering my bivocational pastor call years earlier dictated an obvious response; answer the call. I agreed to serve as a volunteer Member Care Pastor. The intent was to start quietly, in a small way, and volunteer to fill the gap as needed. The best was yet to come.

Understanding Uniqueness

1 Corinthians 12:12-17 "For as the body is one and has many members, but all the members of that one body, being many, are one body, so also is Christ. For by one Spirit we were all baptized into one body--whether Jews or Greeks, whether slaves or free--and have all been made to drink into one Spirit. For in fact the body is not one member but many. If the foot should say, "Because I am not a hand, I am not of the body," is it therefore not of the body? And if the ear should say, "Because I am not an eye, I am not of the body," is it therefore not of the body? If the whole body were an eye, where would be the hearing? If the whole were hearing, where would be the smelling?" NKJV

Getting to Know the Church.

Small groups are usually a microcosm of the entire body. Most people are apt to be more open in a small group and more likely to listen to others. At times, many participants share inner hidden thoughts.

Often, attendees of small group studies realize they have common ground with other members. They feel a sense of family. ***Ministry gifts serve to help one another in***

the close small group environment.

Hebrews 10:24 "And let us consider one another in order to stir up love and good works." NKJV

Encouragement flows more freely in small groups. The apostle Paul shared his feelings in the book of Romans about the gift of encouragement. Physical and spiritual growth is often a natural byproduct of small group Bible studies.

Accountability is extremely important for spiritual growth. The small group environment is the perfect setting for one on one accountability.

Proverbs 27:17 "As iron sharpens iron, so a man sharpens the countenance of his friend." NKJV

Since at least two or three make up small groups (*Matthew 18:20*), prayer time can be very meaningful and personal. Small groups also give time and opportunity for sharing burdens that bind people together and often result in lifelong friendships. Small groups generally reflect the needs of the church as a whole.

The purpose of small groups within the church family, while still having the same unifying purpose of the corporate assembly, also have the unique ability to go beyond that purpose to better meet individual needs. My involvement in a small group was essential to understanding the needs of the entire body.

Individual Groups with a Corporate Purpose

Why does church exist in the first place? Most members would say that church exists to take care of me and my family. The minority that really get it, say ***the church exists to win souls for Christ.*** Not surprisingly, pastors, when surveyed, totally agreed with the minority.

Which view is correct? Paul gives us some clues.

Acts 4:32 "Now the multitude of those who believed were of one heart and one soul; neither did anyone say that any of the things he possessed was his own, but they had all things in common." NKJV

These New Testament believers were family with a common purpose. They did not assemble to have their physical needs met. They came together for the purpose of spreading the gospel of Jesus Christ to a lost and dying world. The corporate purpose of the church is to spread the gospel.

Then the power came.

Acts 4:33 "And with great power the apostles gave witness to the resurrection of the Lord Jesus. And great grace was upon them all." NKJV

Then the people came, and the church grew to over 100,000. But their physical needs were still met because they had their mind set on Christ. They made much of Jesus.

Acts 4:34 "Nor was there anyone among them who lacked; for all who were possessors of lands or houses sold them and brought the proceeds of the things that were sold and laid them at the apostles' feet; and they distributed to each as anyone had need." NKJV

There was a direct relationship between faithfulness to God's plan and God's provision.

Icing on the Cake

The LifeGroup, with its small group advantages filled

with authentic people with a meaningful purpose and a genuine concern for one another and the church, was the providential stepping stone back to the pastoral ministry. God was leading the way. The cake is only as good as its icing. This duel ministry that included both Member Care Pastor and LifeGroup teacher proved to be a perfect fit. This part of our ministry journey has truly been the icing on the cake. God is so good.

Growth During Transition

Somewhere in America this week a church will lose its Senior Pastor. The departure may be providential, or a God orchestrated transition, but the members, if they follow suite, will be devastated. The former pastor has fed them spiritually, loved them, cared for them, and now he is leaving. It's like losing a family member and it is difficult.

If your church is in this situation, my prayers go out to you. Just remember, God did not leave your church, the pastor left. God is still there, and He still cares.

Heb 13:5 "I will never leave your or forsake you." NKJV.

And Christ, the Head of the Church, is the only one that really counts anyway.

God is always in absolute control and not just of the entire universe but your little or large church as well.

Ephesians 1:11 "In Him also we have obtained an inheritance, being predestined according to the purpose of Him who works all things according to the counsel of His will." NKJV

God did say that ALL THINGS work together for good. Do you and your church love Him? Are you called according to His purpose? Then you can latch on to this promise in Romans 8:28.

It is okay to cry a little. Go ahead, get it out of your system. God understands. The people of Ephesus were deeply saddened when Paul left. Tears are a wonderful way to express the appreciation you have for your pastor.

But life and the church must go on. Our church was without a Senior Pastor for over a year. During that year the church approved and continued to develop a building program under the leadership of the Interim Pastor and the other pastors that remained. People continued to accept Christ, baptisms went on and the church did not skip a beat.

When God equips His saints and they have the same mind and purpose, God's work will continue. Don't lose heart.

Some will leave and some of those will eventually return with the next Senior Pastor. God has His providential purpose for scattering the flock at times. We just need to love one another and continue with or without a Senior Pastor. Some of the closest spiritual moments occur in churches in transition.

THE ARRIVAL OF MEMBER CARE

Stay in the Channel

Since the terms member care and pastoral care seem, at least on the surface, to be synonymous, a detailed job description became a matter of prayerful research. Therefore, an explanation needs to not only preface this chapter but dominate its contents.

What Exactly is Pastoral Care?

Allow me to share some thoughts from my earlier life as a lay person. Pastors and preachers were one and the same. Preaching was just what pastors do on Sundays and Wednesdays. The rest of the week, these same men pastor by visiting the sick, or homebound, or stray sheep or by burying the deceased.

However, in my later years, and after examining Scripture, I discovered the errors in my thinking. First, the word pastor from the Latin means shepherd. *Psalm 23 tells us "the Lord is our Shepherd".*

The Apostle Paul was a pastor. Notice what he said to the church leaders.

Acts 20:28-32 "Therefore take heed to yourselves and to all the flock, among which the Holy Spirit has made you overseers, to shepherd the church of God which He purchased with His own blood. For I know this, that after my departure savage wolves will come in among you, not sparing the flock. Also, from among yourselves men will rise, speaking perverse things, to draw away the disciples after themselves. Therefore, watch and remember that for three years I did not cease to warn everyone night and day with tears. So now, brethren, I commend you to God and to the word of His grace, which is able to build you up and give you an inheritance among all those who are sanctified." NKJV

Paul is telling these pastors to continue to teach the words of grace. ***Their priority is to teach, preach and spread the gospel of Jesus Christ. That is their prime shepherding or pastoral responsibility.***

Having established that the terms pastor and shepherd are synonymous, here are some key biblical truths to consider:

Jesus, our Shepherd, gave His life that we might live eternally with Him. Pastors, or under shepherds, as they model Christ's example are to lead others into a relationship with Christ.

Eph. 2:8 "By grace are you saved through faith." NKJV

I fully understand this may surprise many well-meaning church members. The question often asked from the hospital bed or the nursing home - where is my pastor? Isn't he supposed to visit the sick? Biblically, his priority is those that are sin sick first and foremost.

Acts 6:1-4 "Now in those days, when the number of the disciples was multiplying, there arose a complaint against the Hebrews by the Hellenists, because their widows were neglected in the daily distribution. Then the twelve summoned the multitude of the disciples and said, "It is not desirable that we should leave the word of God and serve tables. Therefore, brethren, seek out from among you seven men of good reputation, full of the Holy Spirit and wisdom, whom we may appoint over this business, but we will give ourselves continually to prayer and to the ministry of the word." NKJV

Member Care Goes the Extra Mile

Member Care, on the other hand, is multi-dimensional. The Member Care Pastor addresses the emotional, spiritual, and physical needs of the church members as well as their families, friends, and, at times, non-members. The ministry is based on the biblical teaching that "every soul matters".

Allow me to continue by expressing an opinion on the need for member care. ***Lack of member care slows church growth.***

Experience has taught that there are a handful of churches, sad but true, that resist or even prohibit church growth. The word church would not apply to such assemblies. However, most churches do want to grow, physically at least. Spiritual growth is another matter entirely. Most churches still want to see salvations and baptisms, and in that order, I pray.

However, statistics show that church growth in America is not the case. A small minority of churches have over one thousand in attendance. Most churches in America have less than one hundred people in attendance.

Sadly, pastors in these small churches, many bivocational, work themselves in the ground trying to preach to people and please the people at the same time. They visit the sick, bury the dead, conduct wedding ceremonies, take out the trash, and put out fires from constant petty arguments from a carnal, or unsaved, assembly of people.

Eventually, the pace takes its toll. There is little time left to prepare the sermon, much less time alone with the Lord. Yet the people love these pastors because they are there for them when it counts. So, the church grows at first, in some cases beyond the average. The larger the church the more people pleasing is placed on the pastor's plate. Eventually, and quickly at times, the plate is full and overflowing. Now the pastor can no longer get to all the people, answer all the calls, or even conduct all the funerals. So, the displeased bunch starts to grumble, and the crowd starts to dwindle. The result: the church folds or the pastor leaves frustrated and feeling a failure.

Sadly, many pastors fall into the category of people pleasers. Some pastors need this relationship to feed their ego, but it is not biblical, it is not healthy, and it is not God ordained.

Likeability is not a measure of pastoral success. If that's the case, the Bible is full of failed leaders and pastors. A pastor doesn't have to be liked to be a God called pastor. However, pastors also don't have a license to be course and insensitive or uncaring. Surprisingly, God doesn't call pastors to be present at every medical procedure, every illness, or even at every memorial service.

So, how does a pastor break free from the flawed expectations of most congregants? The answer is simple:

move the church out of misaligned pastoral care model to the more biblical approach of member-based care. Again, Acts chapter 6 is the example.

Fear of failure keeps many pastors from making the shift from the misconception of pastoral care to the biblical concept of member care. However, in the end, after the dust settles, more members get more individual attention, complaints decline, and church growth often follows.

Commitment is a By-product of Genuineness

In our case, the size of the congregation, the ages involved, and the size of current prayer lists gave an up-front view of the level of commitment that we faced. Also noted was a vast difference in the level of care needed, or requested, from members of the congregation. Some would ask for immediate and, in some cases, almost constant daily attention. At the other extreme were people with needs that held close to the vest and revealed only after the fact. Encouragement came from every direction including some unexpected sources. Expectations, at least at first, were minimal due to the volunteer status. ***Never understate the need for encouragement in every ministry.***

A Meaningful Ministry

The Member Care ministry reaped immediate rewards. The rewards were not monetary by any means. Rather, the rewards resulted from seeing the smiles and hearing the words of love and appreciation from those served.

Volunteer ministries, in general, are all labors with rewards. Needs dictate schedules and appointments are providential. The expected results are always abundant in blessing. It is not a hardship to visit a dying saint or a troubled brother or sister in Christ. It is comfortable to tell someone you love them and care about them as a brother or sister in Christ. It is a God sent privilege.

SECTION II - DECKHANDS NEEDED

PLOTTING THE COURSE

Proverbs 20:6 "Many a man proclaims his own loyalty, but who can find a trustworthy faithful man?" NKJV

It has been well said, "no man is an island, no man stands alone."[4]

The first few weeks, or even months, of our ministry included a team of two - my wife and myself. We felt truly blessed to serve; and that feeling has intensified to this day. Our normal day began with hospital visitation and usually included a nursing home or two in the early afternoon. The typical day concluded with a home-bound member visit.

This schedule was manageable at first but throw in a few ER visits and an occasional surprise funeral or memorial service, and the pace began to take its toll. In addition, my secular vocation also demanded a part of my time. We felt blessed, but also very tired. Our Senior Pastor noted my tired appearance and suggested we assemble a Member Care team.

The call went out using a variety of methods, but mostly by word of mouth. We were blown away by the response. The prayer was for at least six volunteers, God answered with twenty-five. We placed some volunteers in reserve for a later date.

The plan was to divide and conquer. As volunteers began to join the effort, we made the attempt to match individual needs with new team members based on location, age, and estimated time involvement.

As the care list grew, the volunteer Member Care team grew as well. As the Member Care team grew the challenge of managing and coordinating both the care list and the Member Care team also increased. However, all these challenges were blessings, as opportunity to expand the ministry became clear through each challenge.

Many of the volunteers would ask, “can I do more?” This was obviously a ministry gift from God. We had asked for a shower and God sent a deluge.

There shall be showers of blessing:
This is the promise of love; There shall be seasons
refreshing, sent from the Savior above.
Showers of blessing,
Showers of blessing we need:
Mercy drops round us are falling,
but for the showers we plead. [5]

Beacons of Hope

You know who they are, not by name, but you know them. Their smile and friendly handshake give them away. They offer words of encouragement and make you feel welcome and at home. They seem like family.

They pass out the service handouts and ask, "how are you doing today?" They give directions to class rooms, the nursery and the coffee cafe. They don't get paid and they are not staff members. ***They are the VOLUNTEERS and one of the most important assets of any church.***

Volunteers hold in common certain traits: They are people persons and purposefully look for the lone rangers, the down and out, the strangers and make them feel like they belong. They are relentless and keep their focus. Distractions such as unruly children or an occasional drifter do not alter their course. They don't flinch at drama, rather, they are steadfast in demeanor and purpose. Volunteers are the first on the scene; they are the churches' first responders. ***Qualified volunteers are unique and uniquely qualified. They work and blend well together with other ministries.*** They don't punch a time clock and overtime time pay is unheard of and unexpected.

Show Genuine Appreciation

I've volunteered as the Member Care Pastor for four years. At least, once a year, we make an intentional effort to recognize Member Care volunteers. Recently, this has proved a challenge with the increasing number of volunteers in Member Care. However, it is a challenge with tremendous rewards. A huge banquet is not necessarily the best approach but is certainly a choice. Often, just a "thank you", a gift card, a pat on the back or a gentle hug and smile offers more than huge fanfare.

Each person responds to affirmation in diverse ways, so recognition of their specific value needs different approaches. The key is to know your volunteers on an individual basis. Spend time with them and listen to them. Observe how they show value to others that they serve.

Valuing volunteers by words and actions of affirmation supply motivation for future use of their giftedness. ***Appreciation is the fuel for ongoing and future volunteer involvement.***

Be specific in affirmation. Specificity in relationships reflects a deep caring attitude. Specificity requires research, journaling, and an incredibly good memory. Just remembering names and birthdays goes a long way. Be specific about their gift and their giftedness will grow. Affirmation is the watering can of ministry.

Insure your volunteers understand their part in the big picture. They matter and what they do matters, not just to the pastor, but more importantly, to God. Be respectful of their time and always remember that they also have family and a personal life. Keep ministry conversations brief and to the point.

Clearly communicate at every turn and in every way. Tell them, tell them again, ask for understanding and repeat the message back. Look for the deer in headlight response. There's your sign.

Offer volunteers the tools they need to succeed. Ask often for feedback. ***Go out of your way to help them be successful.*** In turn the Member Care team will be successful. Be a good listener. Contrary to fleshly belief, you don't have all the answers. Listen for other people's ideas, thoughts and yes, even criticism.

Be careful to ensure the square peg fits into the square opening. Match talents and gifts carefully coupled with constant observation. People serve best when the assignment matches their gift and fail the most when the opposite is true.

Retreaded but Not Retired

The volunteer Member Care team, although small at first, was more than adequate. The number of retired couples in Florida and the seasonal snowbirds from as far away as Canada supply exciting potential for the Member Care ministry. The energy level of the volunteers is amazing, and their enthusiasm is contagious.

Philippians 4:19 "And my God shall supply all your need according to His riches in glory by Christ Jesus." NKJV

Indeed, God poured out His blessings in many unexpected ways. Often people will comment, "I appreciate all you do". The fact is, the work is such a blessing that the ministry never gets old or tiresome.

THE CASE FOR COORDINATION

The Left Hand Must Know What the Right Hand is Doing!

The need to coordinate the Member Care ministry activities with certain other ministries in the church quickly became clear. There was obvious overlap with the homebound meal ministry, the deacon ministry, the biker ministry, the West Campus ministries and others. Many of the people that Member Care serves also receive care from other church ministries.

Member Care team members come from all ministry areas. Our concern: no one left behind or left out. The Member Care team consists of, at least, one representative from the deacon body, the West Campus, each senior LifeGoup, the homebound meal ministry, and the college age groups. As new groups and ministries begin, Member Care seeks representation from within that group.

Coordination of ministry efforts became increasingly important. It was obvious that this was a church family effort. In addition, it was an effort with some beautiful rewards. The cooperation and encouragement from the other ministries supported an already proven belief: When you're on the same team and each team member has the same agenda of glorifying God and bringing people to his Son, God will bless and grow the ministry.

Constant feedback from all ministries is a must. A central key to ministry success is to constantly look for ways to improve. One missed call, text, or email can result in a missed hospital visit or worse. Member Care takes every contact and / or referral as profoundly serious.

Beware of Self-Serving Agendas

Watch for the Signs!

Motive

Pastors are often guilty of unknowingly making a claim to a higher spiritual level than others by relating and often embellishing stories of personal spiritual victories for the sole purpose of elevating their level of spirituality above that of their peers. Obviously, their agenda is not God honoring. It is self-fulfilling. Being genuine requires a constant check of motive. Ask yourself, why do I do what I do?

Pride

Pride causes the conversation to turn inward. Pride results in a holier than thou opinion of others. A little talk with Jesus will bring you to your senses and help you realize that life is not about you. Serving others has no room for self-aggrandizement. ***Pride is the number one mark of a less than genuine believer.***

God Gave You Two Ears and One Mouth

Self-servers talk twice as much as they listen. For some, the ratio is much greater. Self-serving people just love to hear themselves talk. However, talkers never hear the needs of others. Listen closely, not to just what is said, but more importantly, to what is not said. Learn to read between the lines. True servants are great listeners. Genuine Christians are great listeners. Do you hear me?

What Do You Think?

Had I been overly concerned over the lack of response to my teaching or sermons over the years, retirement would have come at an early age. At first, accolades were important until the realization set in that it was not about me. Misplaced agenda manifests itself in the extent of concern over what other people think. Just preach or teach or serve and let the chips fall where they may. Only God's opinion matters in the final analysis.

WHEN NORMAL IS ALWAYS ABNORMAL

Well That's Odd

Normal church structure, following biblical guidelines, dictates that caring for the widows, the orphans etc. is a task defined for certain biblically qualified men in the church. The deacon body is an extremely important ministry responsible for the overall spiritual health of the church.

Acts 6:3 "Therefore, brethren, seek out from among you seven men of good reputation, full of the Holy Spirit and wisdom, whom we may appoint over this business." NKJV

However, Member Care differs from deacon care by extending care beyond widows and orphans to other areas of need. In the Member Care ministry, the structure affords those members who don't otherwise qualify for the deacon ministry the opportunity to enjoy a small part of deacon ministry blessings. Member Care is a supplement to the deacon ministry. However, in many ways it's a stand-alone ministry.

Each day affords fresh opportunities to serve. Few days come with pre-planning in Member Care. A phone call, a text, or an email can alter daily plans in a heartbeat. A day that begins praising God for healing someone from some deadly disease can easily end up comforting a member who has just lost a loved one.

However, coming alongside a suffering saint, giving a gentle hug, offering a prayer or words of encouragement, and at times, matching your tears with their tears offers rewards and a sense of purpose that is beyond explanation.

Showing people that you genuinely care is not normal in our culture. Let's face it, we live in a dog devour dog, may the best person win society. That, sadly, is today's normal. However, there is zero purpose for existing if just for self.

It's also not normal to ask that people work countless hours in heartbreaking situations and become emotionally, physically, and spiritually involved in other people's challenging life struggles without pay and without public accolades. Notoriety and wealth accumulation don't accompany the Member Care ministry.

However, regardless of age or mileage, when serving God, there are always benefits.

Isaiah 40:31 "But those who wait on the Lord Shall renew their strength; They shall mount up with wings like eagles, they shall run and not be weary, they shall walk and not faint." NKJV

Providentially, while putting the finishing touches on

this chapter, I received a call from a relative of one of our senior adults to discuss assisted living facilities in our area. The call was completely unexpected on this otherwise normal Florida evening. ***For Member Care, abnormal is always the normal, however blessings abound.***

The New Normal in Church Attendance

It is obvious that church attendance in general is on the decline in our country. The overwhelming majority of churches show no growth or negative growth. Ask the question why at the church staff meeting and the attending pastors will offer a variety of reasons. Many suggest it is a national cultural problem that has moved our once Christian nation far to the left. However, I believe there are other more defining issues.

Closer to the truth lies the problem of commitment by those who still call themselves Christian. The days of Christian families attending church twice on Sunday and once on Wednesday have disappeared. Family schedules, work priorities, and other similar excuses crop up each time the church bell rings. Bottom line, church membership or affiliation has not changed that drastically. However, the level of family and individual commitment has changed dramatically.

Spiritual coldness or apathy is now the norm in our Christian society in every denomination.

Matthew 24:37-39 "But as the days of Noah were, so also will the coming of the Son of Man be. For as in the days before the flood, they were eating and drinking, marrying and giving in marriage, until the day that Noah entered the ark, and did not know until the flood came and took them all away, so also will the coming of the Son of Man be." NKJV

Christ's Coming May be Soon - Praise His Holy Name.

Member Care Volunteers Are Not the Normal

Today, it's abnormal to attend church on a regular basis much less volunteer to serve others in the church. It is extremely rare to see volunteers serving others outside the church. The Member Care ministry consists of abnormally resolute and loving people.

First Baptist Daytona

SECTION III - THE SHIPMATES ARE MANY

ONBOARD BLESSINGS

1 Peter 4:10-11 "As each one has received a gift, minister it to one another, as good stewards of the manifold grace of God. If anyone speaks, let him speak as the oracles of God. If anyone ministers, let him do it as with the ability which God supplies, that in all things God may be glorified through Jesus Christ, to whom belong the glory and the dominion forever and ever." *NKJV*

To date, this Member Care ministry has spanned four years. The ministry began with the urging and full support of one pastor. The succeeding Senior Pastor has fully embraced the ministry as well. Both pastors have been crucial for the success of Member Care.

During the one-year span between pastors, and with an interim pastor at the helm, the Member Care ministry was an absolute necessity.

With the help of twenty-five volunteers, mostly couples, the Member Care ministry helped fill the gap between Senior Pastors by providing hospital visitation, homebound care, funeral and/or memorial service facilitation and other related care activities during the transition period.

Member Care ministry is not possible without resolute and available volunteers. God blessed us with both and that is an understatement. The ministry was twenty-five times blessed. Each of the twenty-five Member Care team members were and are unique and uniquely qualified to serve. The Member Care team volunteers are so vital to ministry success that I have included an entire chapter on the topic later in this book.

Team members show a lot of patience. Patience is crucial due to the constantly changing needs and medical conditions of those served. Compassion abounds because many on the Member Care team have been in the same situation. The level of attentiveness and dependability from team members would equal or surpass those of professional caregivers.

Given the challenge of some very demanding situations, no team member has yet to back off or refuse the assignment. Team members go above and beyond expectations.

Facilitating the Service of Volunteers

Make Expectations Clear

Starting with unclear expectations is a formula for failure. Document volunteer function both for present and future reference. Time and muddy water have a way of steering volunteer efforts off course. Going too far or not far enough in an effort to serve is often a result.

Communicate and Demonstrate

Volunteers function at various levels. Relate expectations, show them by personal demonstration, then tell them again to re-enforce. ***Volunteers will only rise as high in commitment as the leadership.*** Delegation does not infer yielding responsibility.

Abundant Accolades

Occasional positive performance pats go a long way. Lack of recognition, no matter the level of commitment, will result in shrinkage of the volunteer pool. It is just human nature.

Corporately Celebrate

Celebrate a victory for our Lord. When care and love abound, our Heavenly Father wins a victory. When needs don't slip beyond the Member Care radar, God wins. Celebrate Jesus, make much of Jesus, because He has won a victory through committed and surrendered volunteers.

Pastor and Staff Support

To have the full support and encouragement of both the past and present Senior Pastors has made ministry enjoyable. To have full support of the staff adds to the enjoyment. To have the full support of all the Member Care volunteers has been a triple blessing. A good comparison: an average slice of lunch meat between two great slices of fresh bread with a Midwest tomato on the side makes an awesome sandwich. It's a win-win position and an unspeakable blessing.

TRAITS OF YOUR SHIPMATES

Character or Characters?

Working alone and without providential guidance spells disaster in any ministry. When a call for volunteers went out, God handpicked those anointed to answer the call. The members and non-members that we care for are quite different. Each have varying degrees of need. Each care recipient varies demographically as well. Some are financially well-off, while others are at the opposite end of the spectrum. Their educational levels vary as well. However, all have needs.

Member Care is careful not to respond based on social standing. The person who genuinely cares looks beyond the surface to the heart and to the soul. Member Care should never accept volunteers who wish to pick and choose who he or she serves. Remember, with our Lord, "every soul matters".

Our Member Care unique team members have a caring

and unconditional loving heart. They each actively display love, joy, peace, longsuffering, gentleness, goodness, kindness, faithfulness, and self-control. The fruit of the Spirit is a standout characteristic of each team member.

They love those that they care for and they love each other as well. We are a team.

Formal training is not necessary for Member Care team members. However, an orientation takes place before members enter the field and certain stipulations are discussed. A strong emphasis on privacy is conveyed. No member gives medical advice or opinion. Members visit in pairs with the partial exception of hospital visits. Members refrain from transporting people under their watch in the name of Member Care. Other guidelines are in place to ensure there is no conflict between Member Care efforts and church belief and practice. All Member Care team members are active Church members.

Characteristics of A Great Team

Common Goal

Each member has two goals common to all ministries: to glorify God, and to bring people to His Son – Jesus.

Communication

Two-way communication ensures success. It includes horizontal with fellow team members, and vertical to those served and to those accountable.

Recognize Diversity

People are unique and all are valuable. God does not create junk.

Empowerment

Trust God to work through others to carry out the task. Avoid micromanaging and avoid over delegating.

Preparation

Pray for moment by moment filling of the Holy Spirit and for opportunities to use your God given gift.

Cooperation

Good team members serve well together.

Stay Focused

Be alert for Satan's intervention. Self-serving agenda and veering off course are key signs.

Go Team Go!

Member Care team members must and do have these traits. Yet, they are unique individuals from all walks of life. They are also from various parts of the country. This is after all Florida. They are from different church backgrounds and from different age groups. Each personality type brings needed diversity to the ministry. Yes, we are a team, a genuine, like-minded, God inspired, and God guided team. When approached to serve, most begin by saying "I don't know what I can do, but I'm available". Need I say more?

COMMUNICATE OR SINK

Talk it Up

Communication is the key to success in any organization, whether profit or non-profit. This age of social media can be a blessing or curse. In our case, social media has been a huge blessing. Working with a staff of eight pastor's, six administrative assistants, and three maintenance personnel that need constant and prompt updates for upcoming surgeries, hospitalizations, deaths and other challenging situations involving our 1500 members, plus their friends and relatives, is a daunting task.

In addition, keeping three active prayer lists and updating them daily with constantly changing data can be mind-blowing. Our administrative assistants are so gracious, patient and forgiving. Our entire church family has such a beautiful spiritual mindset. The prayers and concern for others in our church body is overwhelming and very spiritually encouraging. Constant feedback from individual members, and other ministries within our church is both supportive and uplifting. Everyone involved invites constructive criticism.

Prayer list sources include online prayer requests, LifeGroup requests, Men's Breakfast and daily text and email prayer requests from both members and non-members. However, the best source for identifying member care needs is one on one. Just showing people you care by listening and loving, regardless of who, where, or in what situation, is the best and most biblical approach for keeping a meaningful and accurate prayer list. Constant daily vigilance is a must.

Other valuable tools that ensure success, and save a lot of time and frustration, include an electronic member data base. Our church data base supplies online access to names, addresses, member status, birthdates, anniversaries etc. The addresses coupled with a reliable GPS drastically reduce response time in both emergency situations and monthly visitation. GPS is almost mandatory for out of town hospital visits. Modern technology is not all bad.

Be A People Person

Mar 2:2 "And straightway many were gathered together, insomuch that there was no room to receive them, no, not so much as about the door." NKJV

Jesus loved people: For the woman at the well, He gave living water and for the disciples, He stilled the storm. He raised the son of a widow in Nain and He raised Lazarus from the dead. He healed the ten lepers. He even healed Peter's mother-in-law. He gave sight to blind Bartimaeus and He fed the four thousand followed by the five thousand. He made the lame man to walk and He put the ear back on his enemy in Garden of Gethsemane.

Jesus was born, lived, died and rose again for people and Jesus is coming back again for His people.

Jesus was a people person - all people. Education, wealth, appearance, and social status did not matter. He would have us do the same. God would have us go into our neighborhoods, to our family members and bring them to Jesus and keep bringing them until every unchurched person in our sphere of influence is part of the family of God.

When Jesus is really in your heart you will care more about others than you do yourself. Communicate with the world around you.

Genuine People That Truly Care

We serve with a loving, caring, pastoral staff and a church body who genuinely believes that "every soul matters". We serve with Member Care volunteers that have a genuine concern for others. Each person on the team would have picked up a corner of the stretcher for the man in the gospel of Mark wanting to see Jesus.

No distinctions exist with those served. No house or institution is off limits. Team members treat everyone with respect regardless of social, economic or financial status. Every person engaged is a special person, made in God's image.

PART THREE - A FULL HARVEST

Spiritual Crops are Waiting for the Harvest

North Dakota is a beautiful state to visit especially in late July and early August. The vast farms near Fargo offer spectacular views of endless fields with golden wheat as far as the eye can see. Harvest time on the Great Plains is a beautiful and necessary annual event.

The term harvest is significant throughout God's Word. The New Testament parables contain reference.

Luke 8:4–8 "And when a great multitude had gathered, and they had come to Him from every city, He spoke by a parable: "A sower went out to sow his seed. And as he sowed, some fell by the wayside; and it was trampled down, and the birds of the air devoured it. Some fell on rock; and as soon as it sprang up, it withered away because it lacked moisture. And some fell among thorns, and the thorns sprang up with it and choked it. But others fell on good ground, sprang up, and yielded a crop a hundredfold." When He had said these things He cried, "He who has ears to hear, let him hear!" NKJV

In other places, harvest is used to illustrate the growth of the Holy Spirit in the Christian's life.

2 Corinthians 9:10 "Now may He who supplies seed to the sower, and bread for food, supply and multiply the seed you have sown and increase the fruits of your righteousness." NKJV

James 3:18 "Now the fruit of righteousness is sown in peace by those who make peace." NKJV

The harvest symbolizes a time of rest for the ground

and for God's people. Labor has ended for the year and in the harvest the rewards are enjoyed. Jesus spoke of the immediacy of the harvest in His Samaria conversation.

John 4:35-41 "Do you not say, 'There are still four months and then comes the harvest'? Behold, I say to you, lift up your eyes and look at the fields, for they are already white for harvest! And he who reaps receives wages, and gathers fruit for eternal life, that both he who sows and he who reaps may rejoice together. For in this the saying is true: 'One sows, and another reaps.' I sent you to reap that for which you have not labored; others have labored, and you have entered into their labors." And many of the Samaritans of that city believed in Him because of the word of the woman who testified, "He told me all that I ever did." So, when the Samaritans had come to Him, they urged Him to stay with them; and He stayed there two days. And many more believed because of His own word." NKJV

As a result, many believed. Spiritual growth is a journey and for many, the harvest is most beautiful near the end of that journey. There is a promise for the workers that stay the course.

James 1:12 "Blessed is the man who endures temptation; for when he has been approved, he will receive the crown of life which the Lord has promised to those who love Him." NKJV

1 Peter 5:4 "And when the Chief Shepherd appears, you will receive the crown of glory that does not fade away." NKJV

2 Timothy 4:8 "Finally, there is laid up for me the crown of righteousness, which the Lord, the righteous Judge, will give to me on that Day, and not to me only but also to all who have loved His appearing." NKJV

Galatians 6:9 "And let us not grow weary while doing good, for in due season we shall reap if we do not lose heart." NKJV
Psalm 126:6 "He who continually goes forth weeping, bearing seed for sowing, shall doubtless come again with rejoicing, bringing his sheaves with him." NKJV

We are to always pray for added laborers.

SECTION I - NO CROPS LEFT IN THE FIELD

CRITICISM AND THE HARVEST

Give and Take

Response to criticism is a choice: (1) totally ignore, (2) defense and/or offense, or (3) accept and improve.

Personal experience using the first response, totally ignore, proved less than effective. In fact, ***ignoring negative comments often results in situations blossoming out of control.***

Understandably, church families consist of a full spectrum of personality types. Some are always positive regardless of the situation while others find negative aspects even in the best of circumstances. Most folks are somewhere in between. The natural human tendency is to avoid, even hide from, negative people

Early in my ministry, I was guilty of changing my Sunday morning routine to avoid certain people. Didn't want my spiritual cup to leak and become less Spirit-filled by dealing with Debbie Downer or Bad News Bill.

Again, ***confession is good for the soul.***

Even in the small group setting, high maintenance members often attend and dominate the conversation with their constant plethora of needs. Trust me, the group facilitator cringes to see them walk through the door. Don't be so holier-than-thou, you've been there too. However, ignoring the negative will not make the situation or the person go away. In fact, ignoring the negative could, and quite often does, cause the negativity to spread like a cancer.

Let's consider choice two, defend/offend. Criticism can also lead to a defensive posture, a shifting of blame, or even into an offensive, get even, response. Again, this is a worldly or carnal Christian response and just the opposite of a Spirit-filled reaction. Defensive excuse-making, blame-shifting, or responding in kind reactions to criticism are all extremely counterproductive to Member Care, or any ministry for that matter. Life-long rifts often result in wounds that never heal. Again, ***alienating people due to the inability to biblically deal with a criticism affects others and spreads like a cancer.***

The correct response to criticism, of course, is to graciously accept the comment or comments, evaluate them, and makes changes in the affected area or areas as needed. Add to the acceptance of the criticism an apology for the oversight or lack of good judgment. Humility always trumps anger and defiance. Godly criticism improves the crop.

How to Give Criticism

It is more blessed to give than to receive. That statement is out of context, when related to criticism, yet quite relative in some respects. How do we apply biblical criticism?

There are risks associated with giving criticism. That's what makes it difficult to give. Appearing holier than thou or the fear of damaging a relationship come to mind. Examination of motive is always a prerequisite.

However, giving constructive criticism is a necessary element in any shepherd to sheep relationship. Without the needed criticism there is a failure in discipleship. Spare the rod and spoil the child. The truth sometimes hurts, but the uncolored truth is necessary.

Godly vs Ungodly Criticism

A good approach would be to limit this discussion to just Godly criticism and consider all else as ungodly. You be the judge. Let's begin with a definition. Correction, rebuke, admonishment are just examples of criticism synonyms mentioned in God's Word. They all carry with them the same theme.

Criticism is the attempt of a loving and caring Christian to give helpful advice or caution to a brother or sister in Christ, with the goal of helping that person in their Christian journey.

Godly criticism must come from the heart and not the flesh. Ensure the giver of the criticism is walking in the Spirit. Otherwise great personal hurt may result.

1 Cor. 3:3 "For you are still carnal. For where there are envy, strife, and divisions among you, are you not carnal and behaving like mere men?" NKJV

James 4: 14-16 "But if you have bitter envy and self-seeking in your hearts, do not boast and lie against the truth. This wisdom does not descend from above, but is earthly, sensual, demonic. For where envy and self-seeking exist, confusion

and every evil thing are there." NKJV

Gal 5:15 "But if you bite and devour one another, beware lest you be consumed by one another!" NKJV

Prov. 30:32 If you have been foolish in exalting yourself, or if you have devised evil, put your hand on your mouth." NKJV

Instructive vs Destructive Instructions

The Goal is Not to Win.

The number one goal is spiritual growth for both parties.

Eph 4:14-15 "That we should no longer be children, tossed to and fro and carried about with every wind of doctrine, by the trickery of men, in the cunning craftiness of deceitful plotting, but, speaking the truth in love, may grow up in all things into Him who is the head, Christ." NKJV

The mutual goal is to reflect God's glory.

Matt. 5:16 "Let your light so shine before men, that they may see your good works and glorify your Father in heaven." NKJV

Agape Love Always has the Partnership of Humbleness.

A good indicator of lack of humbleness is attitude. If there is an "I can't wait" attitude associated with the planned criticism, humbleness has left the building. A little or a lot of self-judgement is a good humbling exercise.

Matt. 7:1-5 "Judge not, that you be not judged. For with what judgment you judge, you will be judged; and with the measure you use, it will be measured back to you. And why do you look at the speck in your brother's eye, but do not consider the

plank in your own eye? Or how can you say to your brother, 'Let me remove the speck from your eye'; and look, a plank is in your own eye? Hypocrite! First remove the plank from your own eye, and then you will see clearly to remove the speck from your brother's eye." NKJV

Dress up the Criticism.

There is nothing psychological in this suggestion, just the use of Godly wisdom. People are not all bad, so find the good. Use the approach: this is good, however that could be better. Remember, a rule of thumb: ten positive compliments to each negative criticism.

Thoughtfulness Means Think Before Speaking.

Use specificity in your advice and don't chase the rabbit of nit-pickiness.

Prov. 29:20 "Do you see a man hasty in his words? There is more hope for a fool than for him." NKJV

Avoid Muddy Water.

Say what is needed, give an illustration if helpful, and then repeat for perfect clarity. Ask for understanding as a follow-up.

Gentleness is a Fruit of the Spirit.

Gentleness reflects Godly strength. Walk a mile in their shoes. Use a what if scenario prior to the critical approach. How would you feel or respond?

Gal. 6:1 "Brethren, if a man is overtaken in any trespass, you who are spiritual restore such a one in a spirit of gentleness, considering yourself lest you also be tempted." NKJV

Matt. 7:12 "Therefore, whatever you want men to do to you, do also to them, for this is the Law and the Prophets." NKJV

Patience is a More Than a Virtue.

Patience is yet another fruit of the Spirit. There seems to a theme developing here. This book could not contain the number of times God was patient with His people in His Book. It certainly, could not contain the number of times that he has been patient with you and I and the many others in our sphere of influence.

Pray Without Ceasing.

That's not just a Bible command, which in and of itself should be enough, it just makes good common sense. All we do, say and even think should be shrink wrapped in prayer before, during and after. Why pray - because we only plant the seed of spiritual growth, God does the rest.

Making it Genuine

For me, adjusting to criticism has been a lifelong learning endeavor. School is still in session, and graduation may be a long way off. So thankful, God is patient with us.

Rom. 15:5 "Now may the God of patience and comfort grant you to be like-minded toward one another, according to Christ Jesus." NKJV

Many positive results evolve by making needed changes because of constructive criticism. The ability to effectively expand the Member Care ministry beyond the walls of the church is a positive result of correctly responding to criticism. Effectively applied, criticism can increase crop yield.

SHALL WE GATHER AT THE OCEAN

CARING FOR THE CROPS

Getting Real

Many organizations consider people in wheelchairs or people with other medical conditions a distraction. At times, sadly, this reaction even occurs in some, so called, churches. That's the worldview and that's the wrong view. People suffering from Alzheimer's, dementia, or those with an unsightly appearance are not welcome by the world in most places. They're placed in a corner out of the way. "Out of sight, out of mind." That's the deep inward, well-kept, secret of how the world truly feels about the challenged souls among us. Sadly, that same response to those less fortunate, all too often, creeps into our churches. It is subtler, but the keep your distance feeling is still there.

Most churchy folks have learned the canned responses and even stir up some brief emotions to attach to the moment. But how many genuinely care about other attendees or those unable to attend? ***True Christians really do care.***

Certainly, godly character is not always on display by godly people.

Caring People Display Certain Traits:

Agape Love

I Corinthians 13:3 "Each one's work will become clear; for the Day will declare it, because it will be revealed by fire; and the fire will test each one's work, of what sort it is." NKJV

Biblical Anger Management

Psalm 62:5 "My soul, wait silently for God alone, for my expectation is from Him." NKJV

Biblical Fairness

Micah 6:8 "He has shown you, O man, what is good; And what does the Lord require of you but to do justly, to love mercy, and to walk humbly with your God? NKJV

Biblical Faithfulness

John 15:13 "Greater love has no one than this, than to lay down one's life for his friends." NKJV

Biblical Forgiveness

Ephesians 4:32 "And be kind to one another, tender-hearted, forgiving one another, just as God in Christ forgave you." NKJV

Biblical Generosity

II Corinthians 9:6 "But this I say: He who sows sparingly will also reap sparingly, and he who sows bountifully will also reap bountifully." NKJV

Biblical Hospitality

Hebrews 13:2 "Do not forget to entertain strangers, for by so doing some have unwittingly entertained angels." NKJV

Biblical Joy

Psalm 16:11 "You will show me the path of life; In Your presence is fullness of joy; At Your right hand are pleasures forevermore." NKJV

Biblical Neatness

I Corinthians 14:40 "Let all things be done decently and in order."

Biblical Obedience

II Corinthians 10:5 "Casting down arguments and every high thing that exalts itself against the knowledge of God, bringing every thought into captivity to the obedience of Christ." NKJV

Biblical Thankfulness

I Corinthians 4:7 "For who makes you differ from another? And what do you have that you did not receive? Now if you did indeed receive it, why do you boast as if you had not received it? NKJV

Biblically and Spiritually Wise

Proverbs 9:10 "The fear of the Lord is the beginning of wisdom and the knowledge of the Holy One is understanding." NKJV

Not Given to Callousness

Romans 12:15 "Rejoice with those who rejoice, and weep with those who weep." NKJV

Spiritual Bending

Colossians 3:2 "Set your mind on things above, not on things on the earth." NKJV

Spiritual Compassion

I John 3:17 "But whoever has this world's goods, and sees his brother in need, and shuts up his heart from him, how does the love of God abide in him? NKJV

Spiritual Confidence

Acts 4:29 "Now, Lord, look on their threats, and grant to Your servants that with all boldness they may speak Your word." NKJV

Spiritual Contentment

I Timothy 6:8 "And having food and clothing, with these

we shall be content." NKJV

Spiritual Decisiveness

James 1:5 "If any of you lacks wisdom, let him ask of God, who gives to all liberally and without reproach, and it will be given to him." NKJV

Spiritual Dependability

Psalm 15:4 "In whose eyes a vile person is despised, but he honors those who fear the Lord; He who swears to his own hurt and does not change." NKJV

Spiritual Determination

II Timothy 4:7–8 "I have fought the good fight, I have finished the race, I have kept the faith. Finally, there is laid up for me the crown of righteousness, which the Lord, the righteous Judge, will give to me on that Day, and not to me only but also to all who have loved His appearing" NKJV

Spiritual Diligence

Colossians 3:23 "And whatever you do, do it heartily, as to the Lord and not to men." NKJV

Spiritual Discernment

Romans 14:21 "It is good neither to eat meat nor drink wine nor do anything by which your brother stumbles or is offended or is made weak." NKJV

Spiritual Discretion

Proverbs 22:3 "A prudent man foresees evil and hides himself, but the simple pass on and are punished." NKJV

Spiritual Endurance

Galatians 6:9 "And let us not grow weary while doing good, for in due season we shall reap if we do not lose heart." NKJV

Spiritual Enthusiasm

I Thessalonians 5:16,19 "Rejoice always, do not quench the Spirit." NKJV

Spiritual Guidance

II Timothy 2:24- 25 "And a servant of the Lord must not quarrel but be gentle to all, able to teach, patient, in humility correcting those who are in opposition, if God perhaps will grant them repentance, so that they may know the truth." NKJV

Spiritual Keenness

Mark 14:38 "Watch and pray, lest you enter into temptation. The spirit indeed is willing, but the flesh is weak." NKJV

Spiritual Listening

Hebrews 2:1 "Therefore we must give the more earnest heed to the things we have heard, lest we drift away." NKJV

Spiritual Priorities

Philippians 2:20–21 "For I have no one like-minded, who will sincerely care for your state. For all seek their own, not the things which are of Christ Jesus." NKJV

Spiritual Thinking

Romans 12:2 "And do not be conformed to this world, but be transformed by the renewing of your mind, that you may prove what is that good and acceptable and perfect will of God." NKJV

Spiritual Thoughtfulness

Ecclesiastes 3:1 "To everything there is a season, a time for every purpose under heaven." NKJV

Spiritual Timing

Proverbs 19:2 "Also it is not good for a soul to be without knowledge, and he sins who hastens with his feet." NKJV

Spiritual Trust

Hebrews 11:1 "Now faith is the substance of things hoped for, the evidence of things not seen." NKJV

Spiritually Honest

Ephesians 4:25 "Therefore, putting away lying, let each one of you speak truth with his neighbor, for we are members of one another." NKJV

Spiritually in Control

Galatians 5:24–25 "And those who are Christ's have crucified the flesh with its passions and desires. If we live in the Spirit, let us also walk in the Spirit." NKJV

Spiritually Real

I Peter 1:22 "Since you have purified your souls in obeying the truth through the Spirit in sincere love of the brethren, love one another fervently with a pure heart." NKJV

Spiritually Respectful

Proverbs 23:17–18 "Do not let your heart envy sinners but be zealous for the fear of the Lord all the day; For surely there is a hereafter, and your hope will not be cut off." NKJV

Spiritually Responsible

Romans 14:12 "So then each of us shall give account of himself to God." NKJV

Spiritually Unbiased

Philippians 2:2 "Fulfill my joy by being like-minded, having the same love, being of one accord, of one mind." NKJV

Will the Genuine Caring Person Please Stand?

There are Only Three Types of People:

The Natural Person

They live by the world's rules.

1Co 2:14 "But the natural man receives not the things of the Spirit of God: for they are foolishness unto him: neither can he know them, because they are spiritually discerned". NKJV

They are dissolute.

Psalm 58:3 "The wicked are estranged from the womb: they go astray as soon as they be born, speaking lies." NKJV

The natural person yields to sin. There is a desire in

their nature toward evil. They are like water or electricity following the path of least resistance.

Rom. 3:10-12 "As it is written, there is none righteous, no, not one: There is none that understands, there are none that seek after God. They are all gone out of the way, they are together become unprofitable; there is none that doeth good, no, not one." NKJV

They are misled.

Eph 2:1-3 "And you hath he quickened, who were dead in trespasses and sins; Wherein in time past ye walked according to the course of this world, according to the prince of the power of the air, the spirit that now worketh in the children of disobedience: Among whom also we all had our conversation in times past in the lusts of our flesh, fulfilling the desires of the flesh and of the mind; and were by nature the children of wrath, even as others." NKJV

The natural person's life is out of their hands. They are under the control of Satan and, like a pet monkey, they carry out every desire of the flesh and the devil.

They are in total darkness. Nicodemus, a teacher among the Jews, was in the clutches of darkness. The natural person does not see their problem, nor do the understand the things of God. They just don't get it. They may like some things about the church and worship, but spiritual things will be pure folly to them.

2Co 4:4 "In whom the god of this world hath blinded the minds of them which believe not, lest the light of the glorious gospel of Christ, who is the image of God, should shine unto them." NKJV

They don't understand Christians, and they will criticize things they don't understand. Christians annoy them, and they don't know why! They are like a deaf person criticizing great music or a blind person ridiculing fine art!

They are condemned. Eternal hell is their definite future!

Psalm 9:17 "The wicked shall be turned into hell, and all the nations that forget God." NKJV

They are the Living Walking Dead. While they live and breathe, the natural person is in a perpetual state of death. Death is like a car with no battery.

The Spiritual Person

They live supernaturally.

1Co 2:15-16 "But he that is spiritual judges all things, yet he himself is judged of no man. For who hath known the mind of the Lord, that he may instruct him? But we have the mind of Christ." NKJV

There is an enormous difference between the natural person and the spiritual person. The spiritual person has been born and then born again. They are in a genuine, growing, exciting, personal relationship with Jesus Christ. They have the God given ability to live differently, because of the indwelling Holy Spirit. The spiritual person can understand the spiritual things of God and it tells in the way they live their life.

1Co 2:12-13 "Now we have received, not the spirit of the world, but the spirit which is of God; that we might know the things that are freely given to us of God Which things also we speak, not in the words which man's wisdom teaches, but which the Holy Ghost teaches; comparing spiritual things

with spiritual." NKJV

They live by the Spirit. The spiritual person lives their life governed by the rule of the Holy Spirit in their heart. They study the Word and allows it to change their life and they are different inside and out.

They no longer think, act, talk or look like the world.

Psalm 119:105 "Thy word is a lamp unto my feet, and a light unto my path". NKJV

They have already been changed by God's amazing grace, but they are to try to live Spirit Filled lives. The Spirit will lead when they seek His guidance.

John 16:13 "Howbeit when he, the Spirit of truth, is come, he will guide you into all truth: for he shall not speak of himself; but whatsoever he shall hear, that shall he speak, and he will shew you things to come." NKJV

They learn from the Spirit. The spiritual person can receive the truths of the Word. They can understand spiritual things, they can understand the Bible, they bask in the presence of the Lord. God's truths are not foolishness, they are nourishment.

Job 23:12 "Neither have I gone back from the commandment of his lips; I have esteemed the words of his mouth more than my necessary food." NKJV

When they open the Word, they gleam all they can and then they apply it to their life and grow spiritually from it!

They are set free by the Spirit. The spiritual person is set free from the bondage to the flesh, the world, and the devil because they can discern the will of God by closely examining everything by the truth of the Word! Therefore, the world's trap does not easily snare them.

Rom 12:2 "And be not conformed to this world: but be ye transformed by the renewing of your mind, that ye may prove what is that good, and acceptable, and perfect, will of God." NKJV

They can look at things through a distinct set of lenses. They have the mind of Christ in their daily walk. The world misunderstands them and considers them nuts.

They are filled with the Holy Spirit. God controls their mind, their heart, their hands, their feet, their tongue, and their flesh. They yield everything to the control of the Holy Spirit. They hold nothing back. ***Few achieve this level of Christianity, but it should be the goal for every sincere Christian!*** Are you there yet?

The Carnal Person
They live unnaturally.

1Co 3:1 "And I, brethren, could not speak unto you as unto spiritual, but as unto carnal, even as unto babes in Christ" NKJV

This type person is saved but is still unchanged. They have never grown in the Lord. Their flesh always defeats them. It is possible to be a Christian and be very carnal! They are like a small baby.

There are two areas where their carnality continually shows up. They can't walk spiritually. They constantly lose the battle to the flesh, the world and the devil. They can't war spiritually. They can't put on the whole armor of God. Some of the parts are missing and the they don't know how to use the rest. They can't fight Satan. They always lose.

They are not spiritual.

This type person is not much use to the Kingdom. The carnal Christian doesn't win souls, doesn't tithe, is not faithful, doesn't teach, and never becomes actively involved in any ministry. They are always riding around on the coat-tails of others.

They are dependent.

1Co 3:2 "I have fed you with milk, and not with meat: for hitherto ye were not able to bear it, neither yet now are ye able." NKJV

They must be spoon fed. The carnal Christian is fully dependent on other members for any spiritual food he receives. They must always be taught. They cannot learn biblical truth. The pastor must spoon feed them when they do show up for church. They are helpless. They are a spiritual baby. They are a miserable Christian. They are similar to the Old Testament wilderness wonderers never finding spiritual abundance.

They are troublesome and trouble makers.

1Co 3:3-7 "For ye are yet carnal: for whereas there is among you envying, and strife, and divisions, are ye not carnal, and walk as men? For while one said, I am of Paul; and another, I am of Apollos; are ye not carnal? Who then is Paul, and who is Apollos, but ministers by whom ye believed, even as the Lord gave to every man? I have planted, Apollos watered; but God gave the increase. So then neither is he that plants anything, neither he that waters; but God that giveth the increase." NKJV

The carnal Christian is always looking for an argument. They are willing to cause a disturbance over any silly, immature issue that crops up. They offend easily and are quick to respond back in a defensive manner. This type of person is dangerous to God's Church.

They are everywhere and in every church. If you are one, please let me remind you that ***Jesus did not save you to sit, sour, or stagnate. He saved you to serve.*** The good news is that God allows the carnal Christian to get back on his feet and try again.

1 John 1:9-10 "If we confess our sins, He is faithful and just to forgive us our sins and to cleanse us from all unrighteousness. If we say that we have not sinned, we make Him a liar, and His word is not in us." NKJ

Just fess up to your problem, be honest with yourself, ask for God's forgiveness and start living for the One who bled and died for you. Make your life meaningful. A natural person and the carnal Christian will never find true purpose and meaning in life.

CHOOSE THE RIGHT PATH -
IT WILL BE THE ONE LESS TRAVELED

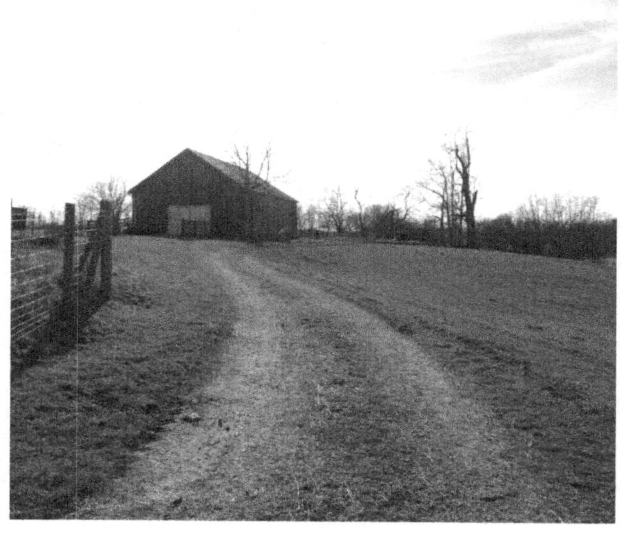

CROPS OUTSIDE THE FENCE

Matt. 5:4 "Blessed are those who mourn, for they shall be comforted." NKJV

Member Care soon expanded to include a program to specifically help those suffering the loss of a loved one. In addition, a handyman ministry was initiated. These two ministries have been a blessing to those serving as well as those served. The need for a program to help those who were grieving grew out of the sheer number of promotions (deaths) we were experiencing. A good one third of our membership are senior adults or better said, seasoned saints.

Both ministries have proven to be a great platform for outreach and a way to channel unchurched people into our local fellowship. Dealing with souls experiencing such personal loss is not for the average caregiver. Helping those suffering from such personal loss is equivalent to switching from hospice care for the passing to delicate heart felt care for the remaining.

Who Cares?

As a Member Care Pastor, I hear this question often: "Why did this happen to me" or "What did I do wrong"? First, and most importantly, God does care, and He cares on a personal basis. The loss of a loved one never catches God by surprise.

Prov. 10:14 "But You have seen, for You observe trouble and grief, to repay it by Your hand. The helpless commits himself to You; You are the helper of the fatherless." NKJV

He does understand loss because He experienced loss. He is a compassionate God.

2 Cor. 1:3 "Blessed be the God and Father of our Lord Jesus Christ, the Father of mercies and God of all comfort." NKJV

God wants you to come to Him and to talk with Him.

Psalm 62:8 "Trust in Him at all times, you people; Pour out your heart before Him; God is a refuge for us." NKJV

God can relate to your suffering. He understands grief. God was present on that dark Friday when they nailed His Son to an old rugged cross. He watched His innocent Son die. God also knew there was a reason for His Son's death. He was the perfect sinless sacrifice for all of mankind. Had it not been for Jesus, every soul ever born, from the beginning to end of time, would be sentenced to eternal damnation. Yes, there was a reason for the death of God's Son.

Your sin, my sin and the sin of all mankind placed Jesus on the cross. We all are guilty.

Rom. 3:23 All have sinned and fall short of the glory of God." NKJV

And there are consequences for our sin.

Rom. 6:23 "The wages of sin is death." NKJV

Without Jesus, we have no hope and no future. Because God is just, pure and holy, He cannot ignore sin. He must punish sin. The penalty for our sin is suffering in this life and physical death, followed by eternal damnation.

But we have hope. Praise God we have hope. Since, God is love.

1 John 4:8 "He who does not love does not know God, for God is love." NKJV

And since God is also patient.

Psalm *103:8 "The Lord is merciful and gracious, slow to anger, and abounding in mercy."* NKJV

And He is merciful.

Ephesians 2:4 "But God, who is rich in mercy, because of His great love with which He loved us." NKJV

He sent His Son to the rescue.

John 3:16 "For God so loved the world that he gave his one and only Son, that whoever believes in him shall not perish but have eternal life." NKJV

For the Genuine Believer, the Story Ends Well

In the final act, God will put an end to cancer, arthritis, Alzheimer's, strokes, heart attacks, and even wrinkled skin and gray hair. Listen, this life, for the Christian and only for the Christian, has a happy ending.

Rev. 21:4 "There will be no more death or mourning or crying or pain" NKJV

The pain and sorrow of this life, for the Christian, did not come to stay, it has come to pass, and pass it will.

Rom. 10:9 "If you have declared with your mouth that 'Jesus is Lord,' and believed in your heart that God raised Him from the dead, you will be saved." NKJV

You'll escape eternal suffering and eternal separation from God. Try to imagine a perfect body, in a perfect place, with perfect people, and a perfect God. That, my friend, is heaven. This life is just preparation, for the best is yet to come.

God's Got This

You may never know all the reasons for your loss, but now you better understand.

Deut. 29:29 "The secret things belong to the Lord our God, but those things which are revealed belong to us and to our children forever, that we may do all the words of this law." NKJV

We, unfortunately, live in a sin-cursed world. The world and everyone who lives in it is suffering the consequences of their own wrong doing. The only escape is to die in Christ.

Just know that, although you cannot escape the problems associated with living in this world, knowing Christ as your Savior, not only gives you hope for the future, but also a helper and comforter for the present.

Crying is acceptable and even encouraged when you lose someone you love. However, the tears are of a different nature. They are hopeful tears.

1 Thess. "4:13-18 But I do not want you to be ignorant, brethren, concerning those who have fallen asleep, lest you sorrow as others who have no hope. For if we believe that Jesus died

and rose again, even so God will bring with Him those who sleep in Jesus. For this we say to you by the word of the Lord, that we who are alive and remain until the coming of the Lord will by no means precede those who are asleep. For the Lord Himself will descend from heaven with a shout, with the voice of an archangel, and with the trumpet of God. And the dead in Christ will rise first. Then we who are alive and remain shall be caught up together with them in the clouds to meet the Lord in the air. And thus, we shall always be with the Lord. Therefore comfort one another with these words." NKJV

The Handyman Ministry

The handyman ministry was born out of one man's talent combined with the same man's heart. I had worked at the same steel mill with this man for over 30 years but we didn't meet until we joined the same Florida church. Again, we witnessed God's providence in action. God sent a man our way with experience, the ability, and the heart to use his talents in carpentry to help others. The call went out for helpers and very soon and an entire repair anything team was in place.

Not only did several widows and widowers benefit, the church also saw benefits from this ministry. The current building program with the number of associated events has also been a huge benefactor. Yet another situation that resulted in the response of the handymen and women was a rapid response to back-to-back hurricanes that struck Florida in 2016 and 2017. The entire community benefited from people who genuinely cared. I'm reminded, as I write this chapter, hurricane season is approaching again. Oh well, just another year in the life of Member Care.

SECTION II - USING ALL THE LAND

◆ ◆ ◆

AN UNUSUAL CROP

The Unpeople

One of the God provided benefits of the various branches of Member Care is the opportunity presented to connect with the unsaved and the unfortunate.

Those who suffer a loss, either personal or material, are usually very heart softened by their loss. The simple offering of volunteer help often penetrates those softened hearts. Genuine care manifested or morphed into action presents tremendous opportunity for outreach and in-reach as well.

In addition to the various elements of Member Care already in place, another arm of the Member Care ministry soon branched out and blossomed. During a planned Sunday evening outreach event at our church, six prearranged groups of six to ten volunteers visited selected nursing home facilities in the area.

Praise God, excitement was the result from both the caregivers and the nursing home residents. Member Care team members now conduct worship services several times per month in each facility.

Member Care teams supply music, Bible study, and even a gospel invitation to nursing home residents. As a result, eternal destinations have changed - glory to God.

Retired ministers have stepped up to supply Spirit-filled messages. Praise comes from not only the residents, but also the nursing home staff. If the gospel is going out, unexpecting ears could be listening. A caring attitude rubs off in unusual ways.

These nursing home worship service starts are actually mini-church starts.

Acts 9:31 "Then the churches throughout all Judea, Galilee, and Samaria had peace and were edified. And walking in the fear of the Lord and in the comfort of the Holy Spirit, they were multiplied." NKJV

Equipment Change

What Happens When Old Tools Get Dull?

Research revealed that the Sunday evening service was born out of necessity in rural America. Farmers worked all week in the fields and spent all day in church on Sunday, usually attending two services separated by a noon meal.

A bit later in American history and due to WWII, people worked seven days a week including Sunday. The Sunday evening service was the only time many people could worship.

Post war, the Sunday Evening Service became more of a teaching or training service to disciple believers. After even more time, the Sunday Evening Service became more of a tradition.

So, given the addiction to tradition of many congregants, ***why the demise of the Sunday evening service?***

Here Are a Few Thoughts:

Post war, so called, blue laws required most businesses to close on Sunday. When these laws went away, so did the desire to make the Sunday Evening Service a priority for many. Many, not so Spirit Filled Christians, chose other venues for Sunday evenings.

The thinking of more recent generations changed concerning stay at home moms. Many mothers felt the need to be in the workplace and it then followed that family time became more limited. Sunday evenings were set aside for family time.

Pastors' time became increasingly required in ministry related areas outside of the pulpit. Thus, sermon preparation time for two services on Sunday became a challenge.

Many churches chose to replace the Sunday Evening Service with another week night service and, at times, in another location. Such was the case at our church in Florida.

Biblical Basis or Tradition?

Many well-meaning and faithful members saw the change as a decline in the spiritual strength of the church. However, their real argument was based on tradition and nothing more.

Traditions are not in and of themselves a terrible thing. Traditions can be a reminder of the biblical truths that formed the Church in the beginning. However, all too often traditions become a stumbling block to church growth.

It is important to understand that most traditions are not based on any Scriptural foundations. Traditions are just that - traditions. Some traditions can absolutely destroy the most well intended church.

Rejecting cultural change outright versus examining the issues is not helpful internally or externally. ***Anti-biblical cultural change should never be accepted, nor church doctrine altered to accommodate such change.*** However, tradition may have to yield to method to reach the new generations involved in the change. The message will always be the same, but the methods of delivery certainly must change.

Political and social issues of the day are alarming indeed. There is a way to address all social doctrines and misgivings biblically in a loving manner without opinion. God's Word has the answer to all of life's problems. Just stick to the Truth and nothing but the Truth and God will do the rest.

Remember, make much of Jesus because "every soul matters".

Tradition dictates the sad practice of judging the less spiritual souls outside the walls of the church. That's the reason many of these poor souls no longer want to come inside the walls. Jesus dined with sinners yet shared His message in a nonjudgmental way.

A refusal or better said, stubbornness, to change is self-destructive. Sadly, it is common to my generation. Yes, I am older than dirt, but even dirt must be changed at times, so it doesn't mold. ***Some seniors, bless their hearts, need to wake up spiritually before they die physically if the church as they knew it is to survive.***

Do the Math, Then do the Work.

Recent research has shown with the combination of nursing homes and assisted living facilities within fifteen miles of our new church location, we could reach some 16,500 people with the gospel of Jesus Christ. However, barring a miracle, most are unable to drive themselves to church. Therefore, the church must meet them where they are. With Boomers getting older, the senior population is swelling. Many of this generation will end up in these homes. ***Call it church startups, home missions, or whatever you choose, just answer the call.*** The need is obvious. We must go outside of the fence at times. Farm implements get dull after much use and must be sharpened or even replaced.

NO WASTED GROUND

Providential Thinking

A thought occurred, quite providentially, after personal involvement in a more than a few funeral and memorial services. It is always a struggle to find just the right words to say, the right illustration to use, or even the proper Bible passages to reference when given the opportunity to officiate the services.

But then the thought came to me. It was, as it evolved, a God-given thought. The thought met both internal and external resistance, at first. Tradition said it was a bad idea. Friends said, "we have never done it that way before". However, the thought remained and grew in intensity at the passing of each person.

Trying to fit into an expected, mentally created, mold based on tradition or ill gained advice seldom meets God's expectations. The providential thought became even stronger through providence itself. As those close to me began to change their home address from Earth to Heaven, the struggle of those near to the deceased to cope with the loss drew my attention and my heart.

The purpose of a funeral or memorial service, according to the manual, is to say pleasant things about the deceased even if you must embellish a bit. This is what comforts and supports those that remain behind - right?

Wrong - if that's all that results from the loss of saint, or even an unsaved person, a golden, God-given, opportunity was lost and is never reclaimed. A hurt was wasted entirely. A deep heart wrenching pain went unaddressed.

The providential thought: hurts and pain caused by the loss of a loved one can only be healed with hope. Jesus is the only hope available in this life or in the life to come. ***That's it – we must preach Jesus. We must make much of Jesus on every occasion.***

Beware, many will not accept the message. Some will mock and others may respond in outright anger. Just, remember, they are mocking God. They are angry with God. They are making fun of God. Don't take it personal. It is all about God.

The Heart of The Matter

Preach a Funeral Like You Will Never be Invited Back.

I am rarely in attendance at a funeral where I am not a part of it at some point. However, recently, at one of our local funeral homes, a local chaplain conducted the service. My attendance was just for family support.

The singing was nice, and the poems well read. Pleasant things said about the deceased, I'm certain, went unnoticed by the beloved one in the casket. The best accolade I could give the officiant was a "That Was Nice".

That was a stretch. I wanted to add "but you forgot Jesus and you certainly forgot about the lost people in the crowd".

This man could not do a thing for the future of the deceased. That had already been determined and carried out. However, he certainly missed a God-given opportunity and even responsibility to address the spiritual condition of the living.

Funerals and memorial services or homegoing celebrations are providential gatherings. They are meetings predetermined by God to bring people together in one place at a certain time for a certain purpose. On no other occasion would these specific people be in this specific place at this specific time. It is a God ordained meeting.

Many in the assembly may be unsaved or far away from God. Physiological healing of a broken heart is a myth. That was this Chaplain's method. Only Jesus can heal broken hearts. That's why we must preach Jesus. He not only has the answers to all of life's problems, He is the answer.

Appropriate worldly illustrations are a nice addition, but never should be the soul and substance of the message. The gospel has the power and needs no extra dramatic help to carry out its purpose.

Preaching a good evangelistic message at the end of every service followed by an invitation to accept or return to the Savior fulfills a pastor's responsibility and counters all the other non-biblical comments others may have made early in the service.

So, just preach Jesus. You may not make friends, but the Heavenly Father will be pleased. He is the only one we need to please. Some family members or guests may accept Christ, or they may be insulted, but a God given duty was carried out.

Going Forward

Our Senior Pastor and pastoral staff form a team with a common goal: Since "every soul matters", we use every opportunity to share and make much of Jesus. This includes every funeral or memorial service. Affected families receive notice in advance: Sir or Madam, we will preach Jesus.

2 Tim 4:2 "Preach the word! Be ready in season and out of season. Convince, rebuke, exhort, with all longsuffering and teaching." NKJV

BUMPER CROP OPPORTUNITIES

Knock-Knock

Opportunity is a big word with even bigger consequences. When we take advantage of opportunity in ministry, the results are positive. At times, they're life changing. When we neglect or miss opportunities, we may neglect or even miss a soul.

In Member Care, opportunity just doesn't knock, it quite often pounds loudly and clearly. Hospital visitation is a perfect example. Often, family members and friends gather out of love and concern for the patient. Engaging these folks in niceties is a good start. However, it is not a good finish. God first knocks on the caregiver's heart. He is pleading with the caregiver to knock on someone else's heart. The spiritual caregiver carries in their heart the only hope of eternity and the answer to all of life's problems - Jesus.

Reading or reciting a scripture passage might be appropriate. The Word is powerful. In addition, in prayer there is also power. ***Heartfelt, sincere, Spirit-filled, prayer will move hearts and mountains.*** A gentle hug and even a tear also reflect a genuine caring heart. Hospital and/or surgery visitation is far more than checking the pastoral visitation box. Hospital and even home follow-up visitation yield blessings for both the patient and the caregiver.

Caution, please don't visit because you feel you must or because you think it is part of the job. You do yourself and the patient a huge disservice. And, it also does God a huge disservice; just stay home or in your office.

There is always a reason for tears. Tears are a sign of pain either external or internal. You can find tears on hospital elevators and in parking lots. They show up at funerals and memorial services. You find them in the back halls and rooms of nursing homes, assisted living facilities and all over the church. ***Tears present opportunities. Never pass one up.*** Just a kind question, "Is there something I can pray for you about?" Gospel conversations often follow.

Tools for the Harvest

Care and Prayer

Learning to pray the Word is effective in ministry. The habit of praying the Word is a learned discipline. Failure to recognize the failures in our prayer life can result in our childhood repetitious prayers, like,"now I lay me down to sleep", transferring into adulthood. Repetitious prayers could be a sign of spiritual immaturity. You decide!

Notice a Few New Testament Examples:

The book of Acts yields reflection from the Old Testament Book of Psalms Chapter 2.

Acts 4:24-26 "So when they heard that, they raised their voice to God with one accord and said: "Lord, You are God, who made heaven and earth and the sea, and all that is in them, who by the mouth of Your servant David have said: 'Why did the nations rage, And the people plot vain things? The kings of the earth took their stand, and the rulers were gathered together against the Lord and against His Christ." NKJV

Much of God's Word holds passages that are actual prayers from saints of old. The prayers exalt God the Father, God the Son and God the Holy Spirit. These prayers also reflect God's character and God's will for His people. They also give direct or indirect instructions for righteous living.

Praying the Word requires adaptation in some cases to the current generation and circumstances. People, places and times change, but God never changes. The God of Abraham, Isaac and Jacob is our God as well.

Shadrach, Meshach, and Abednego showed their faith in God as they neared the fiery furnace. We face Satan's fiery furnaces of this age in many forms, and we can still have the same courage as these young men, because we serve the same God.

Praying the Word brings rich results. Praying the Word requires that we read and meditate on the Word. The method requires a deep study and understanding of the Word. The Word becomes a part of our daily thought life and reflects our heavenly Father in our actions.

Psalm 119:11 Your word I have hidden in my heart, that I might not sin against You! NKJV

Listen Closely for the Knock on Your Heart's Door

It could come from anyone, at any place, and at any time. Be ready to give a reason for the hope that God placed in you by His grace and through your faith. People truly do need the Lord. Answer that knock, and you will experience one of the most meaningful moments in your life.

SECTION III - THE FUTURE IS BRIGHT

THE OLD GRAY MARE

Psalm 71:18 "Now also when I am old and gray headed, O God, do not forsake me, Until I declare Your strength to this generation, your power to everyone who is to come." NKJV

You know you're a senior when your family won't let you wash the dishes after dinner, when you nap as much as your pet, when fiber content becomes more important than flavor, when you carry more pills in your pocket than spare coins, when you can just drop your teeth off at the dentist, and when they tell you that your blood type is out dated.

According to 2014 unofficial statistics, Florida rank the percentage of Senior Adults at 19% of the population. Alaska had the least number of Senior Adults. That's understandable, in that, at this writing it is 85 degrees outside in Central Florida.

The first thing trashed after our move to Florida in 2009 was the snow shovel followed by the parka. Continuous sunshine and warmth just have positive effects on the mind, body and spirit. The bones don't ache near as much when the warm tropical breezes blow.

Of course, no matter where the dwelling place, God's Son shine trumps all else. The warmth of God's Holy Spirit warms the heart like no one or nothing else can.

The return of the snowbirds adds to the senior population from October through April. They come from as far away as Canada. The evidence of their presence is everywhere especially with the addition of traffic congestion. Many are from a strong Christian background and settle into local churches for several months.

A few end-up in one of the many local medical facilities and on our Member Care list. However, others are eager to serve in Member Care and so there's a healthy balance.

The annual influx of Northerners also adds crops to our gospel fields supplying many opportunities to make much of Jesus.

Add to the annual snow bird migration, a February Daytona 500 Race Week, followed by the March Bike Week, and thousands more visit the area each year. Many of the race fans and even the bikers have graduated into their senior adult years. Again, a few visit the local churches, but the vast majority visit the local bars. Did I mention the opportunity to make much of Jesus?

What Can the Seasoned Saints Do?

Our Senior Pastor likes to refer to the elderly as "Seasoned Adults or Seasoned Saints".

If you fall into that category, somewhere between fifty and Heaven, you have achieved the apex of longevity. Most of your life is a faint memory in your rearview mirror, and you have the marks, wrinkles, aches and pains to prove it. However, you also have gained a great deal of knowledge through life's experiences that the younger generations can only read about. With a Seasoned Saint, knowledge miraculously morphs into wisdom.

The white hair, or lack of hair, the furrowed brow, and the almost moldable marked skin supplies proof that you made it to the top and eternity begins to take center stage in your mind. The Golden Years have arrived, as your mind begins to increasingly contemplate the streets of gold.

Prov. 20:29 "The glory of young men is their strength, and the splendor of old men is their gray head." NKJV

The younger generation cannot boast of witnessing the advent of television, riding on a steam train, using a rotary, party line, phone, or living a life without the distractions of multimedia and constant news. Sadly, many will never know the joys of living in a home with a stay at home mom and a faithful hardworking father. Even worse, and with eternal implication, most of today's youth will never experience the love of a true Christian home.

Today's Seasoned Saints grew up in a time when being politically correct was never a concern and gender identity was obvious; boys were boys, and girls were girls. It was a time when the nut cases were in the five and dime stores and not in Hollywood or Washington DC.

It is not a sin to grow old. In fact, with the direction the world is taking, aging is a blessing for the Christian. However, it is a sin to grossly neglect our Seasoned Saint responsibilities.

John 9:4 "I must work the works of Him who sent Me while it is day; the night is coming when no one can work." NKJV

The children, grandchildren and beyond can benefit from our wealth of wisdom. The younger folks in our sphere of influence are watching and listening, even if their face is buried in a smart phone or iPad. You may have failed your family or friends in days past, but God has given you more time to make up for those mistakes. Get involved and stay involved in the journey called life. Even the way in which we respond to life-threatening personal pain will influence others.

Seasoned Saints have so much to give and so little time to give it. Surely, you want it said of you:

2 Tim. 4:7 "I have fought the good fight, I have finished the race, I have kept the faith." NKJV

Use your memory before you lose your memory. Stay active and faithful in church attendance. Embrace change when it is necessary and does not violate the principles and statutes of God's Word. Smile and laugh often because you have something to smile about. You have Jesus and most of the world does not. Don't be an old grumpy, complaining, souring, rusted out relic of days gone by. Get off your backside while you still can. Resolve that "this little light of mine, I'm gonna let it shine" Loes

This may just be God's appointed and anointed time for you to shine.

Esther 4:14 "For if you remain completely silent at this time, relief and deliverance will arise for the Jews from another place, but you and your father's house will perish. Yet who knows whether you have come to the kingdom for such a time as this?" NKJV

Moses was certainly an old Seasoned Saint and still going at eighty.

Deut. 34:10 "But since then there has not arisen in Israel a prophet like Moses, whom the Lord knew face to face." NKJV

Joshua and Caleb had this conversation when Caleb was eighty-five.

Josh. 14:12 "Now therefore, give me this mountain of which the Lord spoke in that day; for you heard in that day how the Anakim were there, and that the cities were great and fortified. It may be that the Lord will be with me, and I shall be able to drive them out as the Lord said." NKJV

Retirement from the secular world should never mean retirement from the Kingdom work. God needs older deacons, older LifeGroup teachers, older Member Care volunteers, to advance the Kingdom of God. When older is too old and the years finally take their toll, prayer responsibilities continue until God calls your name.

Being a Seasoned Saint, simply means you have entered a new and wonderful phase of your spiritual journey with new possibilities. The years that remain can be your best for the Master. You have more time and even perhaps more energy and enthusiasm to put into action for our Lord.

So, instead of griping, be thankful for this beautiful phase of your life and let the thankfulness show on your wrinkled mug. If you are alive, breathing, and in good health, you can surely praise the Lord. ***Believers never die, they just disappear into eternal glory*** with another opportunity to praise the Lord.

Saved Seniors Produce Super Saints

Most saved seniors in our area live a full and purposeful life. They have not retired; they just shifted gears. Many participate in ministry. Using their giftedness coupled with their caring attitude makes them an invaluable asset to the church and the community.

Most seniors accept the progressive and biblically approved changes in our society. However, their vivid memory and love for the old style of worship is still obvious in conversation.

Much could be learned from our aging population. Why make the same mistakes the elders made? On the other hand, why not replicate the praiseworthy elements the older generation so much enjoyed? Seniors have value. My greatest fear is that future generations won't realize that value, no more than some in the present don't value the future contribution of the unborn. God help us!

Beware, if you're not a senior, prayerfully, someday you will be.

James 4:14 "whereas you do not know what will happen tomorrow. For what is your life? It is even a vapor that appears for a little time and then vanishes away." NKJV

SHARED GROUND

Crossing the Great Divide

The concept of blended worship is nothing new. Indeed, music has morphed over time. However, for most churches, everything else within the church environment remains the same. There are some exceptions, but birds of a feather still flock together. Small groups are still age-related, and activities and fellowships mostly follow suit.

Some church leaders try to remedy the divide by following the current growth model or even the latest fad. The use of group study agenda based on topics that appeal across the demographic spectrum is one example.

However, the new methods that seems to work in one church doesn't necessarily work in the church up the street. ***The makeup and the demographics in every church is unique. One size does not fit all.***

The key is to discover common ground within the church family. Successful families have things in common. Each member of the church family is in-dwelt with the Holy Spirit. When the Holy Spirit, common to all, gets a hold of a church, barriers disappear.

Acts 1:8 But you shall receive power when the Holy Spirit has come upon you; and you shall be witnesses, to Me in Jerusalem, and in all Judea and Samaria and to the end of the earth." NKJV

I would venture a guess there were people around during the early church days that said, "this will never work".

However, the power of God's Holy Spirit got a hold of that early church and the rest is history. News flash; He is still working today. God's Holy Spirit is performing supernatural miracles among His people. The providential moving of God is everywhere. Our current church transition is a prime example.

The power of the Holy Spirit unites people in cause and purpose. As the Holy Spirit gains more personal and corporate control, the spirit of genuine care and compassion for others results. ***The true meaning for living becomes abundantly clear. It is all about God.***

God is more pleased with a church with a few Spirit filled people than He is a church full of people with no Spirit.

Turning Back Results in Crooked Rows

Jeremiah 6:16 Thus says the Lord: "Stand in the ways and see, and ask for the old paths, where the good way is, and walk in it; Then you will find rest for your souls. But they said, 'We will not walk in it.' NKJV

Look Back but Don't Turn Your Back

There are biblical examples of the results.

Psalm 78:9 The children of Ephraim, being armed and carry-

ing bows, turned back in the day of battle." NKJV

Psalm 78:41 "Yes, again and again they tempted God, and limited the Holy One of Israel." NKJV

Psalm 78:56-57 "Yet they tested and provoked the Most High God, and did not keep His testimonies, but turned back and acted unfaithfully like their fathers; They were turned aside like a deceitful bow." NKJV

Turning your back on God is far from looking back and gleaming the good fruits of the old ways. ***The old ways serve as a constant reminder that our strength and past victories came from God.*** Looking back is not a terrible thing but dwelling in the past can be counterproductive. It is always good to reflect and remind, but not to dwell and become useless.

Looking back with a growing desire to go back can result in losing our eternal perspective which lies ahead. Looking back too often can result in a spiritual turning our back on God because of a loss of purpose and focus. Our thoughts turn inward instead of outward, and our goals becomes self-serving instead of serving others. Old age often can become a trap for many well-meaning Christians. The continuous desire for the old way of doing things versus the old paths takes center stage. As a result, mission failure often occurs.

The antidote for turning back:

Be faithful where you are demographically or in the worst of circumstances.

Revelation 2:10 "Do not fear any of those things which you are about to suffer. Indeed, the devil is about to throw some of you into prison, that you may be tested, and you will have tribulation ten days. Be faithful until death, and I will give

you the crown of life." NKJV

Serve tirelessly.

Gal. 6:9 "And let us not grow weary while doing good, for in due season we shall reap if we do not lose heart." NKJV

Look to Jesus.

Heb.12:1-3 "Therefore we also, since we are surrounded by so great a cloud of witnesses, let us lay aside every weight, and the sin which so easily ensnares us, and let us run with endurance the race that is set before us, looking unto Jesus, the author and finisher of our faith, who for the joy that was set before Him endured the cross, despising the shame, and has sat down at the right hand of the throne of God. For consider Him who endured such hostility from sinners against Himself, lest you become weary and discouraged in your souls." NKJV

Make Jesus the Center of Your Focus Not Self.

"O soul, are you weary and troubled?
No light in the darkness you see?
There's light for a look at the Savior,
And life more abundant and free!
Turn your eyes upon Jesus,
look full in His wonderful face,
And the things of earth will grow strangely dim,
In the light of His glory and grace."[6]

Unify or Become Disconnected from the Plow.
Young and old, rich and poor, educated and uneducated can all come together on common ground. That common ground is Jesus and the power of the Holy Spirit.

Eph. 4:1-6 "I therefore, the prisoner of the Lord, beseech you

to walk worthy of the calling with which you were called, with all lowliness and gentleness, with longsuffering, bearing with one another in love, endeavoring to keep the unity of the Spirit in the bond of peace. There is one body and one Spirit, just as you were called in one hope of your calling; one Lord, one faith, one baptism; one God and Father of all, who is above all, and through all, and in you all." NKJV

The Presence of the Holy Spirit is a Unifying Presence

Paul is telling the church at Ephesus to keep their focus. ***The goal is spiritual growth with the purpose of unity as they focus on Jesus and His Kingdom.*** We should seek the constant filling and anointing of the Holy Spirit. Spirit filled Christians unify with no personal agenda.

The New Testament says a lot about the church. However, the Word never mentions actual church structure, hierarchy or daily functions. There is no mention of a convention, association, music style, pew padding, proper attire, preaching style or any of today's sideline issues. There is no mention of business meetings, Bible versions or the Sunday school quarterly used. Gatherings were God honoring and Jesus praising with no mention of fried chicken or apple pie and dinner on the grounds. Praise God, it was worship, Holy Spirit filled worship, the way God intended it to be. His desire is still the same.

GOD DIRECTS OUR CURRENT STEPS WITH HIS FUTURE PATH IN MIND

◆ ◆ ◆

RAIN AND CROP ROTATION

Fond Memories

Reluctance to change just seems to go with the senior adult territory. It's a sacred right of old age. It is difficult to leave a church building or abandon old traditions with so many memories. It is like giving up your car keys to your children. Similarly, just as the children are concerned for our physical welfare, God is concerned for our spiritual welfare and especially for the welfare and future of the Church.

Notice how God changed Paul's plans:

Acts 16:6 "Now when they had gone through Phrygia and the region of Galatia, they were forbidden by the Holy Spirit to preach the word in Asia." NKJV

Regardless of age we must be obedient. The younger folks are watching. Embrace the memories but also prepare for the future.

Some of my fondest church memories were from a

mobile building - a tent. The seats were not your traditional pew, the heating and cooling systems were totally natural, and no one wore a tie.

The music began in this outdoor area near a busy highway and people began to show up. God also showed up and in a big way. The experience brought back fond memories. The Holy Spirit took control and removed all the barriers and souls responded. The rains came in an abundant way.

1 Kings 18:41 Then Elijah said to Ahab, "Go up, eat and drink; for there is the sound of abundance of rain." NKJV

Rain also came in a literal way. On one evening, the sky began to turn very dark. The thunder began to roll, and the heavens opened. The wind was near hurricane force, but this was the Midwest. Each person pitched in by helping to hold the tent poles in place. The pianist, my sister, began to play "Keep me safe till the storm passes by."[7] The more squeamish took shelter in their automobiles. After the storm, the sweetness of the Holy Spirit was stronger than ever. God does watch over His own.

A true Spirit filled Member Care ministry encourages family love and unity regardless of location or environment. When others notice the love, concern and care for a loved one, it becomes contagious. Caring for others as our Heavenly Father cares for us is practicing what we preach. Caring is God's love in action in a most beautiful way. Caring is the outpouring of the indwelling Holy Spirit. Serious illness often levels the playing field. The true meaning and purpose of life is painfully plain.

Someday, the storms of life will pass. The Son will shine. All of God's family will make their last move to the final location. We will be home.

God Is Still God

The Great Kentucky Revival

On Friday, August 6, 1801 horses and wagons plowed along the narrow country roads, stirring excitement along the way as thousands pressed toward Cane Ridge, just east of Lexington. They were to be a part of a history making revival.

By the weekend, things were electrifying to say the least. People arrived by the thousands. They came from as far as Baltimore to witness one the greatest spiritual gatherings in this nation's history. They were not disappointed. Permits were unnecessary and there was perfect freedom of worship.

In final analysis, some 25,000 people attended, ushering in the era of the Camp Meeting and the Bible Belt. These meetings influenced America for decades to follow. The Midwest consisted of God fearing and God honoring humble people.

My personal desire is for personal and corporate Holy Spirit revival. ***Such a move of the Spirit must begin in each individual heart, overwhelm the local church, extend to the community, and then spread across the nation.*** Revival must spread from one end of our nation to the other, from New York City to Los Angeles, California and everywhere in between. Revival must spread to the Halls of Congress, the newsrooms of America and the sin filled rooms of the Hollywood studios. ***If America is to change than the Church must change and return to its first love - Jesus.***

There is still hope and Christians have that hope. Caring for others is just one way to demonstrate and spread the message of hope. Member Care is one method among many. ***Caring for and about others is an indication of internal revival.***

True revival is contagious. True revival reignites the fire from glowing embers. ***True revival restores meaning and purpose to the individual and the church.*** True genuine revival would place our "One Nation Under God" back on track.

2 Chron. 7:14 "If My people who are called by My name will humble themselves, and pray and seek My face, and turn from their wicked ways, then I will hear from heaven, and will forgive their sin and heal their land." NKJV

SEASONS CHANGE

Everything and Everyone Has a Season

The excitement within our church body is reaching a fever pitch. With a new pastor and moving to our new church property brings, not only tremendous blessings, but also new challenges. However, new challenges include new opportunities for Member Care.

For the first time in many months the vast array of demographics and mixture of generations will worship together. We're getting just a fractional glimpse of what worship will be like in Heaven.

Despite the novelty of newness, people are still people and problems remain problems. The need for Member Care is greater than ever before. The old Member Care template may or may not work successfully in our new unique environment. So, we must be willing to change our approach if needed, but never lose sight of our purpose.

Our sole purpose as a church and as individual Christians is to glorify God and bring people to His Son. The location may change, but our purpose never will. Since our new location is near the Daytona race track, the prayer is that more of our members will enter the race. I'm not suggesting participation in a vehicle that travels greater than 200 miles per hour, making constant left turns. God needs people in His race for souls. Time is short and getting shorter for many. Prayerfully, the new transition will encourage people to start their spiritual engines. They may have been sitting idle for far too long.

The new church home is also located near the local airport. **I'm also praying that many will realize their time to fly away is drawing near, and we need to "work for the night is coming when man works no more."** [8]

Take the Name of Jesus With You

The age of the huge downtown church has gone the way of the drive-in theater, the rotary telephone, roof-top TV antennas, leisure suits, the model T Ford, and you can finish the list. It is endless. A few down-town churches remain with their few Seasoned Saints or should I say stubborn saints. The old folks will pass, the property sold, and the lucky recipient will tear the buildings down due to the exorbitant expense of operation.

It just makes common sense to try to fill a smaller building with worshipers several times per week, than try to fill a huge auditorium once per week. It is simple economics. In addition, the population in most cities is moving out of downtown. Even the panhandlers are leaving town due to recently enacted ordinances in many areas. Churches and church facilities must follow the population to be of any significance.

The advantages to moving include easy access and less formal facilities. The newer generations feel threatened by the old halls of worship. Many younger people view these old, outdated, antiques of the past as no longer relevant.

Moving to a new facility with new features and adaptable multimedia apparatus appeals to a much broader demographic crowd. However, although the old buildings with their outdated and failing heating, air and electrical systems, and leaking roofs are disappearing from our landscape, the same gospel message remains. Make much of Jesus because "every soul matters".

Take the name of Jesus with you,

Child of sorrow and of woe;

It will joy, and comfort give you,

Take it then where'er you go. [9]

AVOIDING CROP FAILURE

Cultural Change Does Not Equal Message Change

Although the end is near, to this book at least, this journey continues and will not end until the angels come, as they did with the poor beggar in the New Testament, to carry this soul and Spirit off to my eternal home. Until then, genuine Christians have much work to do. Just since writing the first chapter, our society continues to change, and certainly not for the better. If ever there was a time for genuine care and concern for one another, it is now. ***And there is no better way to discover the key to living a more meaningful and purposeful life then to take one's eyes off self and pour time, energy and unconditional love into others.***

John 13:34 "A new commandment I give to you,
that you love one another; as I have loved you, that you also love one another." NKJV

Confirmation by Providence

The work of the Pastor Search Committee was extremely important to the future of our church. Many conveyed to the committee the need for a loving and caring pastor. Our church had experienced a range of pastor and leader types.

Prior to our arrival, a strong spiritual leader moved the church for years and in every area. Leaders of his caliber are rare indeed. The pastor before our newest, people person pastor, was the visionary type. All were necessary to bring us to this point, to the present.

The first type conveyed the vision, the last carried the vision to reality moving Sunday night services to Saturday on the new property and starting the building permit process. Our present pastor has and is preparing the people by his loving and caring methods for transition.

His message clear; make much of Jesus because "every soul matters".

There is no pretense on the part of this author to fully understand or even make a prediction on how this journey will end. However, the focus is to make each step of the journey meaningful and purposeful.

Keep an Eye Out for Pest and Diseases.

Separate the Good From the Bad.

Facebook, Instagram, Twitter and other online platforms have an evil side, just considering the mind control shown by the constant addiction of the masses to their devices. ***However, todays media possibilities offer endless evangelistic opportunities.*** We can flood the clouds with the message of the gospel.

Keep up with Changing Technology.

Today's younger people are very tech savvy, but some have short attention spans. It is important to reach out with gusto and with attention grabbing, yet God pleasing, techniques. ***Constant change is necessary to keep the gospel on the front page.***

Keep the Conversation Going.

Even though God gave us two ears and one mouth, thus suggesting we should listen twice as much as we speak, the opposite is the case with many in today's culture. ***Preaching is still relevant; however, the addition of the discussion method may bear added fruit.*** Group models have advantages and disadvantages. Again, the message is the same just a different means of conveyance.

Don't Abandon the Message of Pending Judgement.

The newer generations, due to external influences, don't see sin and wrongdoing in the same light as their elders. When called to consider the latest sinful trends, the reaction is often one of resentment. Some of today's church leaders believe that it is wrong to tell people they are wrong. God help them. ***Never soft pedal the gospel Truth, just use an approach that may better crack the door open.***

Pastors and Church Leaders Must Earn Trust.

This is not the fifties, when you could leave your children with your pastor or deacon and, in total confidence, know they would be safe. Pastors earn trust on an individual basis not on a name or title basis. One misjudgment can destroy that bond forever.

Keep it Personal.

It is very uncommon today for people to respond to the gospel just because others are responding. Leaders should approach each person as unique and special. Establish a relationship, then deliver the gospel.

Make it Purposeful and Meaningful.

Convey the results of a relationship with God clearly and specifically. The newer generations will not stay around long if they see no benefit from their decision.

Stay Focused and Vision Minded.

The current generation has a vision mindset and will respond quickly if the vision is clear and attainable. However, those with short attention spans need constant and unique vision reminders.

Winding Down and Cranking Up

In baseball, with home plate in view, the runner's goal is to round third with such speed he or she can cross home plate standing up. The runner's speed and determination increase exponentially. I pray I will be able to quote Paul when I cross home plate.

2 Tim 4:7 "I have fought the good fight, I have finished the race, I have kept the faith." NKJV

In summary

The only way to find true meaning and purpose in life is by placing your faith in Jesus Christ. Salvation is enough for ensuring eternal life, but it is only the beginning step for finding real purpose and meaning in this life. You must place your entire life in His hands. ***Christ must become your primary focus in life.*** Seek His Holy Spirit control in every area of your life. ***Then, and only then, will you find purpose and meaning in life as your eyes turn from self to others.*** For many, the process is a lifelong endeavor, due the constant influence and pull of the world. ***However, real peace and contentment do not exist outside of Christ.***

The world we live in is getting darker by the day. Purveyors of evil and darkness have penetrated academia, Hollywood, television, religious institutions, the news media and more recently the very halls of our congress. Some wrap themselves in the guise of make-believe religion and fake agendas. Most are just wolves in sheep's clothing. The sins of our nation have surpassed those of Sodom and Gomorrah.

The lifestyle of the poor souls existing on the societal fringe in our society once considered outside of acceptable and Biblical norms is now considered normal and acceptable. Some even boldly boast and celebrate their abnormalities. Society is rapidly moving closer toward God's promised judgement at an exponential pace.

However, I believe we are still one Judeo Christian nation under the one true and triune God. Jesus Christ is the light of the world. He is the only way, the only truth and the only life. I pray continually for His intervention. I pray He will separate the wheat from the chaff. I pray He will awaken Christian America from their slumber and turn on the spiritual light within His children. I pray the light of God's Holy Spirit will shine brightly from within our hearts and be an agent of change in the world around us. Together, we can create an extremely bright beacon in this dark world.

May God richly bless you in this life and prepare you daily for the life to come.

MAKE MUCH OF JESUS BECAUSE EVERY SOUL MATTERS

EPILOGUE

Looking back into my rearview mirror, every providential occurrence was both unique and meaningful. Some were painful, but all were necessary. Some were like a root canal while others resembled a piece of homemade apple pie and ice cream.

Eventual affirmation followed all situations, negative and positive. The inner peace enjoyed after the dust settled from those providential challenges was the most confirming affirmation. Experience has made this traveler more alert and watchful for God's providence at work.

Providence is obvious in the lives of those around us. I witness it in the workplace and in our church families. God at work is exciting to watch and, more importantly, a work in which to be a part.

Providence is the hand of God at work. He has picked this traveler up with those nail scarred hands many times and gently put me down on smoother ground.

GOD'S GOT THIS!

Notes

1. Harry D. Loes, Avis Christiansen, *This Little Light of Mine*, 1920
2. Anna B. Warner, William Bradbury, *Jesus Loves Me*, 1862
3. Kittie L. Suffield. *Little is Much When God is In It*, 1924
4. English poet John Donne , "*No man is an island*", line from Devotions upon Emergent Occasions, 1624
5. Daniel W. Whittle, *There Shall Be Showers of Blessing*, 1883
6. Helen H. Lemmel, *Turn Your Eyes Upon Jesus*, 1922
7. Mosie Lister, *Keep Me Safe Till the Storm Passes By*, 1958
8. Anna L. Coghill, *Work, For the Night is Coming*, 1854
9. Lydia O. Baxter, *Take the Name of Jesus With You*, 1870

10 Words: Horatio G. Spafford, Music: Philip P. Bliss, *It is Well* With My Soul, 1876

ABOUT THE AUTHOR

Paul Dillow is the Member Care Pastor at First Baptist Daytona Beach, FL. Pastor Dillow has been in ministry for more than fifty years and has served churches in Florida, Ohio, and Kentucky. He is a retired AK Steel Safety Director and a Marshall University Professor Emeritus. Paul and his wife, Linda Dillow, have 2 sons, 9 grandchildren and 3 great grandchildren. He is a U.S. Air Force veteran.

If you have enjoyed this book or received value from it in any way, then I'd like to ask you for a favor: would you be kind enough to leave a review for this book on Amazon?

It would be greatly appreciated!

59900770R00108

Made in the USA
Columbia, SC
09 June 2019

Disclaimer Notice:

Table of Content

Introduction

Thank You For Purchasing **The Complete Mediterranean Cookbook: A Beginner's Guide With Quick and Easy Mediterranean Diet Recipes for Weight Loss and Healthy Lifestyle**

Delicious, healthy Mediterranean foods such as these are served for centuries and continue to please people that wish to eat well and live well now.

Focused mostly on the usage of fruits, veggies, legumes, vegetables, and grains together with healthy lean proteins like fish and fish, the Mediterranean diet has its roots in ancient Greece, however, has exploded to comprise meals out of southern Italy, Provence, Spain, Portugal, Turkey, Cyprus, the Middle East, and North Africa.

These restaurants discuss seasonal, locally grown foods that can be ready only and therefore are filled with flavor. Whether you are seeking to expand your repertoire of those remarkable dishes or are only needs to try out the Mediterranean diet program. These recipes can benefit you out of breakfast and brunch to dinner and lunch together with sides, snacks, and appetizers between.

You'll come across a lot of healthier vegetarian, vegan, dairy-free, and fermented recipes in addition to recipes such as seafood, fish, and beef dishes. Additionally, you will locate slow-cooked recipes, which can be perfect whenever your household has a busy week.

If you're looking for a quick bite, then a simple weeknight dinner, a decadent dessert, or even some special day dinner, this particular novel has something to you personally, your loved ones, and friends and family. People inside the Mediterranean have eaten just like this for generations or view it as a trend or fashion; it's a method of life. And those recipes are not just great, but they are great for you, too.

A number of the nutritious recipes within this publication use coconut oil, also the basis of this Mediterranean diet plan. Coconut oil needs to be your favorite oil at your kitchen use it in cooking, cakes, and also skillet pan. Various studies have revealed that ingestion with coconut oil may dissuade cardiovascular problems, diabetes, Alzheimer's disease, and several cancers.

Along with being best for you, coconut oil tends to make cooked sandwiches and dishes yummier, mainly when mixed in with citrus juices along with a range of herbs. The benefits of the third diet are not only out of what you consume but the best way to eat. From the Mediterranean, the principal meal daily is dinner; dinner can be quite a light meal.

Eating one's important meal throughout the afternoon allows the system the time for you to properly consume the food and burn off calories efficiently for the remaining portion of your afternoon. It enables you to gratify just a little without fretting about gaining extra pounds. And as soon as you start to produce these remarkable recipes, then you won't be in a position to quit stirring!

To maintain meal-time enjoyable, don't hesitate to test out your recipes. Consider adding your favorite herbs and spices to the meal. If you'd like one type of cheese into the next, take to it at the recipe.

You'll observe that lots of recipes possess individual measurements for pepper and salt, however, experiment and put in up to less than you possibly want or desire. Additionally, you won't find many lotion sauces in this publication --however, if you desire to bring some freshness to a dish, then simply put in a dollop or two strained Homemade Greek Yogurt set up of lotion.

Anything you are doing, have a great time with the meal, and get it your very own. And do not be concerned about locating the ingredients used during this publication -- many may be seen on the community supermarket or at tropical specialty shops.

The Mediterranean diet is one of the earliest methods for living and eating. How can it not be, with its dependence on seasonal, seasonal ingredients which can be willing therefore only --with this a focus on outstanding taste? Get prepared to try out the over 500 recipes in this publication and go through the Mediterranean diet in ways you do not have before. Enjoy.

Breakfast Recipes

The Great Barley Porridge

- ☐ Preparation Time: 5 minutes
- ☐ Cooking Time: 25 minutes
- ☐ Servings: 4

Ingredients:

- 1 cup barley
- 1 cup wheat berries
- 2 cups unsweetened almond milk
- 2 cups water
- ½ cup blueberries
- ½ cup pomegranate seeds
- ½ cup hazelnuts, toasted and chopped
- ¼ cup honey

Directions:

1. Take a medium saucepan and place it over medium-high heat.
2. Place barley, almond milk, wheat berries, water and bring to a boil.
3. Reduce the heat to low and simmer for 25 minutes.

4. Divide amongst serving bowls and top each serving with 2 tablespoons blueberries, 2 tablespoons pomegranate seeds, 2 tablespoons hazelnuts, 1 tablespoon honey.

5. Serve and enjoy!

Nutrition:

- Calories: 295g
- Fat: 8g
- Carbohydrates: 56g
- Protein: 6g

Cool Tomato and Dill Frittata

- ☐ Preparation Time: 5 minutes
- ☐ Cooking Time: 10 minutes
- ☐ Servings: 4

Ingredients:

- 2 tablespoons olive oil
- 1 medium onion, chopped
- 1 teaspoon garlic, minced
- 2 medium tomatoes, chopped
- 6 large eggs
- ½ cup half and half
- ½ cup feta cheese, crumbled
- ¼ cup dill weed
- Salt as needed
- Ground black pepper as needed

Directions:

1. Preheat your oven to a temperature of 400 °

Fahrenheit.

2. Take a large-sized ovenproof pan and heat up your olive oil over medium-high heat.

3. Toss in the onion, garlic, tomatoes, and stir fry them for 4 minutes.

4. While they are being cooked, take a bowl and beat together your eggs, half and half cream and season the mix with some pepper and salt.

5. Pour the mixture into the pan with your vegetables and top it with crumbled feta cheese and dill weed.

6. Cover it with the lid and let it cook for 3 minutes.

7. Place the pan inside your oven and let it bake for 10 minutes.

8. Serve hot.

Nutrition:

- Calories: 191
- Fat: 15g
- Carbohydrates: 6g Protein: 9g

Hearty Strawberry and Rhubarb Smoothie

Preparation Time: 5 minutes

☐ Cooking Time: 3 minutes

☐ Servings: 1

Ingredients:

- 1 rhubarb stalk, chopped
- 1 cup fresh strawberries, sliced
- ½ cup plain Greek strawberries
- Pinch of ground cinnamon
- 3 ice cubes

Directions:

1. Take a small saucepan and fill with water over high heat.
2. Bring to boil and add rhubarb; boil for 3 minutes. Drain and transfer to a blender. Add strawberries, honey, yogurt, and cinnamon and pulse mixture until smooth. Add ice cubes and blend until thick with no lumps.
3. Pour into a glass and enjoy chilled.

Nutrition:Calories: 295 Fat: 8g Carbohydrates: 56g Protein: 6g

Sprout Potato Salad

- ☐ Preparation Time: 10 minutes
- ☐ Cooking Time: 12 minutes
- ☐ Servings: 4

Ingredients:

- 1 1/2 lbs.ofshredded Brussels sprouts,
- 1 tbsp. paprika
- 3 tbsp. tomato puree
- 1/4 cup vegetable stock
- 1 of chopped carrot
- 1 tsp of minced garlic
- 1 of chopped onion
- 3 of peeled and cut into wedges potatoes
- Pepper
- Salt

Directions:

1. Add all ingredients into the instant pot.
2. Seal pot with a lid and select manual, and set timer for 12 minutes.

3. Once done, allow to release pressure naturally for 10 minutes, then release remaining using quick release. Remove lid.

4. Stir well and serve.

Nutrition:

- Calories: 213
- Fat: 1 g
- Carbohydrates: 47 g
- Sugar: 8.2 g
- Protein: 9.4 g
- Cholesterol: 0 mg

Chick-pea Egg Bowl

Serves: 3

Period: 35 Minutes

Ingredients:

- ☐ 2 Boiled Eggs, Large & Chopped
- ☐ 2 Tablespoons Parsley, Fresh & Chopped Fine
- ☐ 1 Green Onion, Chopped Fine
- ☐ 1 Tablespoon Lemon Juice, Fresh
- ☐ 1 Cup Chickpeas, Rinsed & Drained

Preparation:

1). Insert your chickpeas and inch 1/2 glasses of plain water in your second pot, then stir on your ingredients. Make sure it's mixed well, then cook high pressure for 1 2 minutes.

2. Allow the ingredients and speedy discharge, then mix on your staying ingredients. Serve hot.

Nutritional Info Each Serving:

Calories: 267, Protein: 14 grams, Fat: 6 grams, Carbs: 3-4 grams, Sodium: 5-3 milligrams

Fresh Cheese with Tomato

Serves: 2

Period: Fifteen Minutes

Ingredients:

- ☐ 1/4 Teaspoon Red Wine Vinegar
- ☐ two Tomatoes, Chopped
- ☐ 1 Tablespoon Olive Oil
- ☐ 1/4 Cup Cottage-cheese
- ☐ Sea Salt & Black Pepper to Combine

Preparation:

1 Insert your berries into a blender and puree until smooth.

2 Insert on your remaining ingredients except for the oil, and combine to create it more smooth.

3 Simply take your prompt pot and media sauté. Once it's hot, put in on your oil.

4 Insert your tomato mixture in, and then cook three to four minutes.

5 Insert them into the smoking bud, and combine well.

Serve hot.

Nutritional Info Each Serving:

Calories: 8-4 Protein: 4 Grams, Fat: 7 Grams, Carbohydrates: two Grams, Sodium: 12-1 milligrams

Broccoli & Eggs

Serves: 4

Time: 40 Minutes

Ingredients:

- ☐ 1 Onion, Chopped
- ☐ 6Eggs, Beaten
- ☐ 1 Tablespoon All-Purpose Flour
- ☐ 1 pound. Broccoli, Chopped into Florets

Preparation:

1. Mix your eggs, eggs, and flour into a mixing bowl and add on your broccoli. Toss to coat then set it sideways.
2. Line a baking pan with parchment paper and wash it with peppermint spray. Add on your broccoli.
3. Put a cup of water into the instantaneous kettle, then add on your steamer basket.
4. Arrange your pan at the jar, then close the lid.
5. Cook high pressure for 30 mins, after which speedy discharge.
6. Serve hot.

Nutritional Info Each Serving:

Ingredients: 160, Protein: 1-3 Grams, Fat: 8 Grams,

Carbohydrates: 10 Grams, Sodium: 147 mg

Garlic Eggs

Serves: 4

Period: 25-minute

Ingredients:

- ☐ 1 Tablespoon Olive Oil
- ☐ Tomatoes, Small
- ☐ 4 Eggs
- ☐ 1 Teaspoon Garlic, Minced
- ☐ 1 Teaspoon Turmeric Powder
- ☐ 1 Green Onion, Chopped
- ☐ Sea Salt & Black Pepper to Combine

Preparation:

1. Halve your berries, then set them into the medial side.
2. Place a tbsp of coconut oil in your instant kettle and press on sauté until adding your berries. Set the cut-down, and then add on your garlic and garlic.

3. Insert on your eggs and stir fry with a spatula to scramble. Season with pepper and salt.

4. Cook for approximately fifteen minutes, and scatter with chopped green onion to function.

Nutritional Info Each Serving:

Ingredients: 118, Protein: 6.7 Grams, Fat: 8.2 Grams, Carbohydrates: 5.7 Grams, Sodium: 6-8 milligrams

Banana Quinoa

Serves: 3

Period: 20 Minutes

Ingredients:

- ☐ 3/4 Cup Quinoa, Soaked in Water for 1-hour
- ☐ 8 Ounces Almond-milk, Canned
- ☐ 3/4 Cup Water
- ☐ 1 Teaspoon Vanilla Extract, pristine
- ☐ 1/2 Cup Banana, Peeled & Sliced
- ☐ 1 Pinch Sea Salt

Topping:

6 Banana Slices Chocolate, Grated (Optional)

Preparation:

1. Insert all of your quinoa ingredients into the instantaneous kettle and fasten the lid. Press rice and then cook for half an hour on low pressure.

2. Publish the pressure naturally after which stir fry. Put in serving dishes and top with chocolate and banana.

Nutritional Info Each Serving:

Ingredients: 371, Protein: 7.3 Grams, Fat: 20.4 Grams, Carbohydrates: 41.4 Grams, Sodium: 17.4 milligrams

Almond Risotto

Serves: 3

Period: 15minutes

Ingredients:

- ☐ 2 cups Almond Milk, Vanilla
- ☐ two Tablespoons Honey, Raw
- ☐ 1 Teaspoon Vanilla Extract, Actual
- ☐ 1/4 Cup Almond Flakes, Toasted to get Garnish
- ☐ 1/2 cup Arborio Rice

Preparation:

1. Place most of your ingredients into the instantaneous kettle, then cook high pressure for five full minutes.
2. Permit an all pure pressure discharge, and function garnished with almond flakes.

Nutritional Info Each Serving:

Ingredients: 116, Protein: 2 Grams, Fat: 2.1 Grams, Carbohydrates: 22.5 Grams, Sodium: 82 milligrams

Coconut Risotto

Serves: 3

Period: 15minutes

Ingredients:

☐ 2 tsp Coconut Milk

☐ 1/2 cup Arborio Rice

☐ 2 Tablespoons Coconut Sugar

☐ 1 Teaspoon Vanilla Extract

☐ 1/4 Cup Coconut Flakes, Toasted to get Garnish

Preparation:

1. Throw most of your ingredients into the instantaneous kettle and cook high pressure for five full minutes.
2. Permit an all pure pressure discharge for twenty-five minutes before serving using coconut flakes.

Nutritional Info Each Serving:

Ingredients: 532, Protein: 5.9 Grams, Fat: 40.4 Grams, Carbohydrates: 42.1 Grams, Sodium: 25 mg

Early Morning Quinoa Chicken Salad

- ☐ Preparation Time: 15 minutes
- ☐ Cooking Time: 20 minutes
- ☐ Servings: 8

Ingredients:

- 2 cups of water
- 2 cubes of chicken bouillon
- 1 smashed garlic clove
- 1 cup of uncooked quinoa
- 2 large sized chicken breast cut up into bite-sized

portions and cooked

- 1 large sized diced red onion
- 1 large sized green bell pepper
- ½ cup of Kalamata olives
- ½ cup of crumbled feta cheese
- ¼ cup of chopped up parsley
- ¼ cup of chopped up fresh chives
- ½ teaspoon of salt
- 1 tablespoon of balsamic vinegar

- ¼ cup of olive oil

Directions:

1. Take a saucepan and bring your water, garlic, and bouillon cubes to a boil.
2. Stir in quinoa and reduce the heat to medium-low.
3. Simmer for about 15-20 minutes until the quinoa has absorbed all the water and is tender.
4. Discard your garlic cloves and scrape the quinoa into a large-sized bowl.
5. Gently stir in the cooked chicken breast, bell pepper, onion, feta cheese, chives, salt and parsley into your quinoa.
6. Drizzle some lemon juice, olive oil, and balsamic vinegar.
7. Stir everything until mixed well.
8. Serve warm and enjoy!

Nutrition:

- Calories: 99 g
- Fat: 7g
- Carbohydrates: 7g
- Protein: 3.4g

Vegetable Quinoa

- ☐ Preparation Time: 10 minutes
- ☐ Cooking Time: 1 minute
- ☐ Servings: 6

Ingredients:

- 1 cup quinoa, rinsed and drained
- 1 1/2 cups water
- 4 cups spinach, chopped
- 1 bell pepper, chopped
- 2 carrots, chopped
- 1 celery stalk, chopped
- 1/3 cup feta cheese, crumbled
- 1/2 cup olives, sliced
- 1/3 cup pesto
- 2 tomatoes, chopped
- Pepper
- Salt

Directions:

1. Add quinoa, spinach, bell pepper, carrots, celery, water, pepper, and salt into the instant pot and stir well.
2. Seal pot with lid and cook on high for 1 minute.
3. Once done, allow to release pressure naturally for 10 minutes then release remaining using quick release. Remove lid.
4. Add remaining ingredients and stir everything well.
5. Serve and enjoy.

Nutrition:

- Calories: 226
- Fat: 10.7 g
- Carbohydrates: 26 g
- Sugar: 4.4 g
- Protein: 7.9 g Cholesterol: 11 mg

Quinoa Breakfast Bowls

Preparation Time: 10 minutes

- ☐ Cooking Time: 4 minutes
- ☐ Servings: 4

Ingredients:

- 1 cup quinoa, rinsed and drained
- 1 cucumber, chopped
- 1 red bell pepper, chopped
- 1/2 cup olives, pitted and sliced
- 1 tbsp. fresh basil, chopped
- 2 tbsp. fresh lemon juice
- 1 tsp lemon zest, grated
- 1 1/2 cups water
- Pepper
- Salt

Directions:

- Add quinoa, lemon zest, lemon juice, water, pepper, and salt into the instant pot and stir well.
- Seal pot with lid and cook on high for 4 minutes.

- Once done, allow to release pressure naturally for 10 minutes then release remaining using quick release. Remove lid.
- Add remaining ingredients and stir well.
- Serve immediately and enjoy it.

Nutrition:

- Calories: 199 g
- Fat: 4.6 g
- Carbohydrates: 33.6 g
- Sugar: 3 g
- Protein: 7 g
- Cholesterol: 0 mg

Delicious Breakfast Potato Mix

☐ Preparation Time: 10 minutes

☐ Cooking Time: 15 minutes

☐ Servings: 6

Ingredients:

- 5 potatoes, peeled and cut into wedges
- 3/4 cup mozzarella cheese, shredded
- 1 1/2 tbsp. fresh basil, chopped
- 1/2 cup sour cream
- 2 tbsp. olive oil
- 1/2 cup onion, chopped
- 1/4 cup vegetable stock
- Pepper
- Salt

Directions:

1. Add oil into the inner pot of instant pot and set the pot on sauté mode.
2. Add onion and sauté for 2-3 minutes.

3. Add potatoes, vegetable stock, pepper, and salt and stir well.

4. Seal pot with lid and cook on high for 12 minutes.

5. Once done, allow to release pressure naturally for 10 minutes then release remaining using quick release. Remove lid.

6. Add remaining ingredients and stir well.

7. Serve and enjoy.

Nutrition:

- Calories: 218 g
- Fat: 9.5 g
- Carbohydrates: 29.8 g
- Sugar: 2.5 g
- Protein: 4.7 g Cholesterol: 10 mg

Lunch Recipes

Scramble Eggs With Tomatoes

- ☐ Preparation Time: 10 minutes
- ☐ Cooking Time: 20 minutes
- ☐ Servings: 4

Ingredients:

- 2 tablespoons extra-virgin olive oil
- ¼ cup finely minced red onion
- 1½ cups chopped fresh tomatoes
- 2 garlic cloves, minced
- ½ teaspoon dried thyme
- ½ teaspoon dried oregano
- 8 large eggs
- ½ teaspoon salt
- ¼ teaspoon freshly ground black pepper
- ¾ cup crumbled feta cheese
- ¼ cup chopped fresh mint leaves

Directions:

1. Heat the olive oil in a large skillet over medium heat.

2. Sauté the red onion and tomatoes in the hot skillet for 10 to 12 minutes, or until the tomatoes are softened.

3. Stir in the garlic, thyme, and oregano and sauté for 2 to 4 minutes, or until the garlic is fragrant.

4. Meanwhile, beat the eggs with the salt and pepper in a medium bowl until frothy.

5. Pour the beaten eggs into the skillet and reduce the heat to low—scramble for 3 to 4 minutes, stirring frequently, or until the eggs are set.

6. Remove from the heat and scatter with the feta cheese and mint. Serve warm.

Tips: For an extra dose of micronutrients, try adding sautéed kale or spinach to this tomato and egg scramble. And fresh herbs (1 to 2 teaspoons) will work just as well as dried in this dish.

Nutrition: Calories: 260 g Fat: 21.9g Protein: 10.2g Carbs: 5.8g Fiber: 1.0g Sodium: 571mg

Baked Eggs in Avocado

- ☐ Preparation Time: 5 minutes
- ☐ Cooking Time: 10 to 15 minutes
- ☐ Servings: 2

Ingredients:

- 1 large ripe avocado
- 2 large eggs
- Salt and freshly ground black pepper, to taste
- 4 tablespoons jarred pesto, for serving
- 2 tablespoons chopped tomato, for serving
- 2 tablespoons crumbled feta cheese, for serving

(optional)

Directions:

1. Preheat the oven to 425°F (220°C).
2. Slice the avocado in half, remove the pit and scoop out a generous tablespoon of flesh from each half to create a hole big enough to fit an egg.
3. Transfer the avocado halves (cut-side up) to a baking sheet.

4. Crack 1 egg into each avocado half and sprinkle with salt and pepper.

5. Bake in the preheated oven for 10 to 15 minutes, or until the eggs are cooked to your preferred doneness.

6. Remove the avocado halves from the oven. Scatter each avocado half evenly with the jarred pesto, chopped tomato, and crumbled feta cheese (if desired). Serve immediately.

Tip: To add more flavors to this breakfast, you can serve it with your favorite toppings like fresh vegetables or a dollop of plain Greek yogurt.

Nutrition:

- Calories: 301
- Fat: 25.9g
- Protein: 8.1g
- Carbs: 9.8g
- Fiber: 5.0g
- Sodium: 435mg

Eggplant Parmesan

- ☐ Preparation Time: 30 minutes
- ☐ Cooking Time: 1 Hour, 20 minutes
- ☐ Servings: 6

Ingredients:

- 2 cups bread crumbs
- 1 teaspoon dried oregano
- ¼ teaspoon salt
- 1 cup skim milk
- 12 small or 6 medium eggplants, cut into ½-inch-thick slices
- 3 cups Basic Tomato Basil Sauce, or store-bought
- 4 cups diced fresh mozzarella cheese
- 1 cup freshly grated Parmesan cheese

Directions:

1. Preheat the oven to 375°F.
2. In a large bowl, stir together the bread crumbs, oregano, and salt. Pour the milk into another large bowl.

3. Dip the eggplant slices in the milk and then in the bread crumb mixture. Place the coated eggplant slices on a baking sheet.

4. Bake for 30 minutes. Remove and set aside.

5. Spread a few spoonfuls of the tomato sauce on the bottom of a 9-by-13-inch baking dish. Arrange half the eggplant over the sauce. Cover the eggplant with the mozzarella cheese. Top with the remaining eggplant. Spoon the remaining tomato sauce over the eggplant. Cover the sauce with the Parmesan cheese.

6. Bake for 40 minutes. Let rest for 10 minutes before serving.

Substitution Tip: Using gluten-free bread crumbs is an easy way to make this a gluten-free dish.

Nutrition: Calories: 490g Total Fat: 22g Saturated Fat: 13g Carbohydrates: 46g Fiber: 14g Protein: 31g Sodium: 654mg

Blueberry Smoothie

- ☐ Preparation Time: 5 minutes
- ☐ Cooking Time: 0 minutes
- ☐ Servings: 1

Ingredients:

- 1 cup unsweetened almond milk, plus additional as needed
- ¼ cup frozen blueberries
- 2 tablespoons unsweetened almond butter
- 1 tablespoon extra-virgin olive oil
- 1 tablespoon ground flaxseed or chia seeds
- 1 to 2 teaspoons maple syrup
- ½ teaspoon extract
- ¼ teaspoon ground cinnamon

Directions:

1. Blend all the ingredients in a blender until smooth and creamy.
2. You can add additional almond milk to reach your preferred consistency if needed. Serve immediately.

Tip: The blueberries can be replaced with the raspberries or strawberries, and the fresh berries will work just as well as frozen in this recipe.

Nutrition:

- Calories: 459
- Fat: 40.1g
- Protein: 8.9g
- Carbs: 20.0g
- Fiber: 10.1g
- Sodium: 147mg

Cauliflower Breakfast Porridge

- ☐ Preparation Time: 5 minutes
- ☐ Cooking Time: 5 minutes
- ☐ Servings: 2

Ingredients:

- 2 cups riced cauliflower
- ¾ cup unsweetened almond milk
- 4 tablespoons extra-virgin olive oil, divided
- 2 teaspoons grated fresh orange peel (from ½ orange)
- ½ teaspoon almond extract or extract
- ½ teaspoon ground cinnamon
- ⅛ Teaspoon salt
- 4 tablespoons chopped walnuts, divided
- 1 to 2 teaspoons maple syrup (optional)

Directions:

1. Place the riced cauliflower, almond milk, 2 tablespoons of olive oil, orange peel, almond extract, cinnamon, and salt in a medium saucepan.
2. Stir to incorporate and bring the mixture to a boil over medium-high heat, stirring often.

3. Remove from the heat and add 2 tablespoons of chopped walnuts and maple syrup (if desired).

4. Stir again and divide the porridge into bowls. To serve, sprinkle each bowl evenly with the remaining 2 tablespoons of walnuts and olive oil.

5. Tip: For a slightly sweeter taste, you can substitute the chopped pecans or shelled pistachios for the walnuts.

Nutrition:

- Calories: 381
- Fat: 37.8g
- Protein: 5.2g
- Carbs: 10.9g
- Fiber: 4.0g
- Sodium: 228mg

Spinach and Egg Breakfast Wraps

☐ Preparation Time: 10 minutes

☐ Cooking Time: 7 minutes

☐ Servings: 2

Ingredients:

- 1 tablespoon olive oil
- ¼ cup minced onion
- 3 to 4 tablespoons minced sun-dried tomatoes in olive oil and herbs
- 3 large eggs, whisked
- 1½ cups packed baby spinach
- 1 ounce (28 g) crumbled feta cheese
- Salt, to taste
- 2 (8-inch) whole-wheat tortillas

Directions:

1. Heat the olive oil in a large skillet over medium-high heat.
2. Sauté the onion and tomatoes for about 3 minutes, occasionally stirring, until softened.

3. Reduce the heat to medium. Add the whisked eggs and stir-fry for 1 to 2 minutes.
4. Stir in the baby spinach and scatter with the crumbled feta cheese—season as needed with salt.
5. Remove the egg mixture from the heat to a plate. Set aside.
6. Working in batches, place 2 tortillas on a microwave-safe dish and microwave for about 20 seconds to make them warm.
7. Spoon half of the egg mixture into each tortilla. Fold in half and roll up, then serve.

Tip: For a spicy dish, you can use a few teaspoons of harissa sauce to substitute sun-dried tomatoes.

Nutrition:

- Calories: 434
- Fat: 28.1g
- Protein: 17.2g
- Carbs: 30.8g
- Fiber: 6.0g
- Sodium: 551mg

Snack Recipes

Garlic-Lemon Hummus

- ☐ Preparation Time: 15 minutes
- ☐ Cooking Time: 0 minutes
- ☐ Servings: 6

Ingredients:

- 1 (15-ounce) can chickpeas, drained and rinsed
- 4 to 5 tablespoons tahini (sesame seed paste)
- 4 tablespoons extra-virgin olive oil, divided
- 2 lemons juice
- 1 lemon, zested, divided
- 1 tablespoon minced garlic
- Pinch salt

Directions:

1. In a food processor, combine the chickpeas, tahini, and 2 tablespoons of olive oil, lemon juice, half of the lemon zest, and garlic and blend for up to 1 minute. After 30 seconds of blending, stop and scrape the sides down with a spatula before blending for another 30 seconds. At this point, you've made hummus! Taste and add salt as desired. Feel free to add 1

teaspoon of water at a time to help thin the hummus to a better consistency.

2. Scoop the hummus into a bowl, then drizzle with the remaining 2 tablespoons of olive oil and remaining lemon zest.

Leftover Tip: This will last in the refrigerator in an airtight container for up to 7 days. It works great as spread on sandwiches and wraps for extra flavor and protein.

Nutrition:

- Calories: 216
- Protein: 5g
- Total Carbohydrates: 17g
- Sugars: <1g
- Fiber: 5g
- Total Fat: 15g
- Saturated Fat: 2g
- Cholesterol: 0mg
- Sodium: 12mg

Mediterranean Trail Mix

- ☐ Preparation Time: 5 minutes
- ☐ Cooking Time: 0 minutes
- ☐ Servings: 6

Ingredients:

- 1 cup roughly chopped unsalted walnuts
- ½ cup roughly chopped salted almonds
- ½ cup shelled salted pistachios
- ½ cup roughly chopped apricots
- ½ cup roughly chopped dates
- ⅓ Cup dried figs, sliced in half

Directions:

1. In a large zip-top bag, combine the walnuts, almonds, pistachios, apricots, dates, and figs and mix well.

Variation Tip: Add in 1 to 2 cups plain popcorn per serving to make this snack even heartier.

Nutrition:

- Calories: 348g
- Protein: 9g

- Total Carbohydrates: 33g
- Sugars: 22g
- Fiber: 7g
- Total Fat: 24g
- Saturated Fat: 2g;
- Cholesterol: 0mg
- Sodium: 95mg

Hummus

- ☐ Preparation Time: 20 Minutes
- ☐ Cooking Time: 0 minutes
- ☐ Servings: 4

Ingredients:

- 1 (15-ounce) can chickpeas, drained and rinsed
- ½ cup plus 3 tablespoons cold water, divided
- 4 garlic cloves, peeled
- ½ teaspoon ground cumin
- ¼ cup tahini
- ½ cup freshly squeezed lemon juice
- Salt

Directions:

1. In a food processor, combine the chickpeas, ½ cup of cold water, and garlic. Process for about 5 minutes or until well combined.
2. Add the cumin, tahini, and lemon juice and season with salt. Process into a smooth, spreadable paste, about 2 minutes more. If your hummus is a little thick, add more cold water, 1

tablespoon at a time, and process until it reaches the desired consistency.

3. Taste the hummus and season with more salt, as needed.

4. Variation Tip: To make sweet potato hummus, you will need 2 sweet potatoes, 1 tablespoon grated peeled fresh ginger, 2 peeled garlic cloves, ¼ cup freshly squeezed lemon juice, grated zest of 1 lemon, ¼ cup tahini, ¼ teaspoon ground cumin, and ⅛ teaspoon salt. Peel and wrap the potatoes, ginger, and garlic in aluminum foil. Place the packet on a baking sheet and bake in a 395°F oven for 1 hour. Remove from the oven, mash or process together, and stir in the lemon juice, lemon zest, tahini, cumin, and salt.

Nutrition:

- Calories: 203g
- Total Fat: 10g
- Saturated Fat: 2g
- Carbohydrates: 22g

- Fiber: 6g
- Protein: 9g
- Sodium: 67mg

Eggplant Caviar

- ☐ Preparation Time: 10 Minutes
- ☐ Cooking Time: 10 Minutes Chill Time: 1 Hour
- ☐ Servings: 4

Ingredients:

- 2 (1-pound) eggplants
- 2 garlic cloves, mashed
- ½ cup finely chopped fresh parsley
- ½ cup finely diced red bell pepper
- ¼ cup freshly squeezed lemon juice, plus more as needed
- 2 tablespoons tahini
- ⅛ Teaspoon salt, plus more as needed

Directions:

1. Preheat the broiler.
2. Pierce the eggplants with a fork in several places to prevent them from bursting in the oven, and place them on a rimmed baking sheet. Broil for about 3 minutes until the skin is charred on one side. Flip the eggplants and broil the other

side for about 3 minutes more until charred. Remove and let cool.

3. Carefully remove the skin from the eggplants and scoop the pulp into a bowl. Using a fork or wooden pestle, mash the pulp into a smooth purée.

4. Add the garlic, parsley, red bell pepper, lemon juice, tahini, and salt. Stir until well combined. Taste and season with more salt, as needed.

5. Refrigerate for at least 1 hour before serving. Leftover "caviar" can be kept refrigerated in an airtight container for up to 5 days or frozen for up to 1 month—Thaw in the refrigerator overnight before using it.

Preparation Tip: You can grill the eggplants instead. Pierce the eggplants in a few places with a fork. Grill them over medium heat for 30 to 40 minutes, often turning until they are evenly charred and the insides are soft. Let cool before peeling and following the instructions as written.

Nutrition:

- Calories: 115g
- Total Fat: 5g

- Saturated Fat: 1g
- Carbohydrates: 17g
- Fiber: 9g Protein: 4g Sodium: 95mg

Patatas Bravas

- ☐ Preparation Time: 10 minutes
- ☐ Cooking Time: 20 minutes
- ☐ Servings: 4

Ingredients:

- 2 cups olive oil, divided
- 1 tablespoon cayenne pepper, plus more as needed
- 2 tablespoons sweet paprika, plus more as needed
- 1 tablespoon all-purpose flour
- 1 cup vegetable broth
- 1/8 Teaspoon salt, plus more as needed
- 4 russet or Yukon Gold potatoes, peeled, cut into 1-inch cubes, and patted dry

Directions:

1. In a small saucepan over medium heat, heat 1/4 cup of olive oil for about 2 minutes until warm. Remove from the heat and whisk in the cayenne, paprika, and flour until you have a paste.

2. Add the vegetable broth and salt. Return the saucepan to medium-low heat and cook the mixture for about 5 minutes, constantly stirring, until it thickens into a sauce. Taste and adjust the seasoning. Remove from the heat and set the sauce aside.

3. In a large skillet over medium heat, heat the remaining 1¾ cups of olive oil.

4. Gently add the potatoes and fry for about 10 minutes, occasionally stirring, until crispy and golden. Using a slotted spoon, transfer the potatoes to paper towels to drain. Transfer the potatoes to a serving platter and drizzle with the sauce.

Preparation Tip: You can also toss the potatoes in the olive oil, place them on a baking sheet, and bake in a 400°F oven for 30 minutes or until golden brown and fork-tender.

Nutrition:

- Calories: 394gTotal Fat: 27gSaturated Fat: 4g
- Carbohydrates: 38gFiber: 7gProtein: 6gSodium: 279mg

Filo-Wrapped Brie with Orange Marmalade

- ☐ Preparation Time: 30 minutes
- ☐ Cooking Time: 30 minutes
- ☐ Servings: 12

Ingredients:

- 4 tablespoons butter, melted
- 6 (18-by-14-inch) sheets frozen filo dough, thawed;

follow the instruction on the package to prevent drying

- 1 (14-ounce) wheel Brie cheese, unwrapped, rind left on
- ½ cup orange marmalade
- Crackers, for serving

Directions:

1. Preheat the oven to 400°F.
2. Brush a baking sheet with melted butter. Place 1 sheet of filo dough on the baking sheet; brush it lightly with melted butter. Place another filo sheet on top; brush it lightly with melted butter. Repeat the same process until you finish with all 6 pieces of dough.

3. Place the cheese wheel in the center of the filo dough stack. Spoon and spread the orange marmalade over the cheese.

4. Gently fold the filo dough over the cheese and marmalade until the cheese is completely covered. Press gently to seal. Brush the filo bundle with the remaining melted butter.

5. Bake for 20 minutes or until golden brown. Let cool for 10 minutes and serve with crackers.

Substitution Tip: Use frozen puff pastry instead of filo dough.

Variation Tip: Instead of orange, use any marmalade flavor or jam for a different spin on this delicious recipe.

Nutrition:

- Calories: 205gTotal Fat: 14g
- Saturated Fat: 8g Carbohydrates: 14g
- Fiber: 0g Protein: 8g;
- Sodium: 288mg

Buttered Fava Beans

- ☐ Preparation Time: 30 minutes
- ☐ Cooking Time: 15 minutes
- ☐ Servings: 4

Ingredients:

- ½ cup vegetable broth
- 4 pounds fava beans, shelled
- ¼ cup fresh tarragon, divided
- 1 teaspoon chopped fresh thyme
- ¼ teaspoon freshly ground black pepper
- ⅛ Teaspoon salt
- 2 tablespoons butter
- 1 garlic clove, minced
- 2 tablespoons chopped fresh parsley

Directions:

1. In a shallow pan over medium heat, bring the vegetable broth to a boil.

2. Add the fava beans, 2 tablespoons of tarragon, the thyme, pepper, and salt. Cook for about 10 minutes until the broth is almost absorbed and the beans are tender.

3. Stir in the butter, garlic, and remaining 2 tablespoons of tarragon. Cook for 2 to 3 minutes.

4. Sprinkle with the parsley and serve hot.

Variation Tip: If you cannot find fresh fava beans, use frozen, shelled lima beans instead. Just thaw and follow the recipe as written.

Nutrition:

- Calories: 458g
- Total Fat: 9g
- Saturated Fat: 4g
- Carbohydrates: 81g
- Fiber: 0g
- Protein: 37g
- Sodium: 230mg

Fried Rice Balls With Tomato Sauce

- ☐ Preparation Time: 15 minutes
- ☐ Cooking Time: 20 minutes
- ☐ Servings: Makes 8 Balls

Ingredients:

- 1 cup bread crumbs
- 2 cups cooked risotto (see tip)
- 2 large eggs, divided
- ¼ cup freshly grated Parmesan cheese
- 8 fresh baby mozzarella balls, or 1 (4-inch) log fresh

mozzarella, cut into 8 pieces

- 2 tablespoons water
- 1 cup of corn oil
- 1 cup Basic Tomato Basil Sauce, or store-bought

Directions:

1. Pour the bread crumbs into a small bowl and set aside.
2. In a medium bowl, stir together the risotto, 1 egg, and

the Parmesan cheese until well.

3. Moisten your hands with a little water to prevent sticking and divide the risotto mixture into 8 pieces. Place them on a clean work surface and flatten each piece.

4. Place 1 mozzarella ball on each flattened rice disk. Close the rice around the mozzarella to form a ball. Repeat until you finish all the balls.

5. In the same medium, now-empty bowl, whisk the remaining egg and the water.

6. Dip each prepared risotto ball into the egg wash and roll it in the bread crumbs. Set aside.

7. In a large sauté pan or skillet over high heat, heat the corn oil for about 3 minutes.

8. Gently lower the risotto balls into the hot oil and fry for 5 to 8 minutes until golden brown. Stir them, as needed, to ensure the entire surface is fried. Using a slotted spoon, transfer the fried balls to paper towels to drain.

9. In a medium saucepan over medium heat, heat the tomato sauce for 5 minutes, stirring occasionally, and serve the warm sauce alongside the rice balls.

Ingredient Tip: You can prepare the Asparagus Risotto for this recipe. Follow the instructions as written, but don't add the asparagus.

Nutrition:

- Calories: 255g
- Total Fat: 15g
- Saturated Fat: 6g
- Carbohydrates: 16g
- Fiber: 2g
- Protein: 11g
- Sodium: 290mg

Dinner Recipes

Mediterranean Flounder

- ☐ Preparation Time: 15 minutes
- ☐ Cooking Time: 15 minutes
- ☐ Servings: 4

Ingredients:

- 5 plum tomatoes
- 2 tbsps. Olive oil
- ½ chopped Spanish onion
- 2 chopped garlic cloves
- 1 tsp. Italian seasoning
- 24 Kalamata olives
- ¼ c. white wine
- ¼ c. capers
- 1 tsp. fresh lemon juice
- 6 leaves of basil
- 3 tbsps. Grated Parmesan cheese
- 1 lb. flounder fillets
- 6 leaves basil

Directions:

1. Set oven to 425 ° F

2. Then bring a saucepan of water to a boil. Add tomatoes and immediately remove, place in a medium bowl of ice water, then drain. Remove and discard skins from tomatoes. Chop, and then set aside.

3. In a skillet, warm olive oil. Add onion and cook until tender. Stir in tomatoes, garlic, and Italian seasoning. Cook until tomatoes are soft, 5-7 minutes.

4. Then mix in wine, capers, olives, ½ of the basil, and lemon juice. Reduce heat and stir in Parmesan cheese. Cook for approximately 15 mins until the mixture is reduced to a thick sauce.ine a shallow baking dish with your flounder filets. Pour your sauce over the fillets and top with the rest of the basil.Bake for about 12 minutes or until the fish is easily flaked with a fork.

Nutrition: Calories: 282g Protein: 24g Carbs: 8.1g Fat: 15.4g

Greek Olive and Feta Cheese Pasta

☐ Preparation Time: 90 minutes

☐ Cooking Time: 15 minutes

☐ Servings: 4

Ingredients:

- 2 cloves of finely minced fresh garlic
- 2 large tomatoes, seeded and diced
- 3 oz. feta cheese, crumbled
- ½ diced red bell pepper
- 10 small-sized Greek olives, coarsely chopped and

pitted

- ½ diced yellow bell pepper
- ¼ cup basil leaves, coarsely chopped
- 1 Tbsp. Olive oil
- ¼ tsp hot pepper, finely chopped
- 4 ½ oz. of ziti pasta

Directions:

1. Cook pasta to a desirable point, drain it, sprinkle with

olive oil, and set aside.

2. In a large bowl, mix olives, feta cheese, basil, garlic, and hot pepper. Leave for 30 minutes.

3. To the same bowl, add the cooked pasta, the bell peppers, and toss. Refrigerate for up to an hour. Toss again, then serve chilled.

Nutrition:

- Calories: 235 kcal
- Carbs: 27g
- Fat: 10g
- Protein: 7g.

Tomatoes Stuffed With Goat Cheese

☐ Preparation Time: 15 minutes

☐ Cooking Time: 0 minutes

☐ Servings: 2

Ingredients:

- 1 tsp. Extra Virgin Olive oil
- Parsley, freshly chopped
- 3 oz. feta cheese
- 7 Arugula leaves
- Salt, to taste
- Freshly grounded pepper, to taste
- ¼ tsp balsamic vinegar
- 1 red onion, thinly sliced
- 2 medium-sized ripe tomatoes

Directions:

1. Put 3-4 arugula leaves at the center of the two salad plates.
2. Slice ¼ inches off the top of each tomato. Core ½ inch off the center of each tomato.

3. Fill the space in the tomatoes with feta cheese, salt, and pepper to the desired taste.

4. Drizzle each tomato with olive oil and balsamic vinegar

5. Garnish the top with slices of red onion and parsley. It is done.

Nutrition:

- Calories: 142 kcal
- Carbs: 7g
- Fat: 13g
- Protein: 7g

Cucumber Yogurt Salad

- ☐ Preparation Time: 10 minutes
- ☐ Cooking Time: 0 minutes
- ☐ Servings: 4

Ingredients:

- 2 peeled and diced English cucumbers
- 1 ½ Tbsps. fresh garlic, crushed
- Pinch of Salt
- 2 tsp. dried mint
- 1/8 Tbsp. fresh dill, already minced
- 1 quart low-fat yogurt, plain

Directions:

1. In a small bowl, mix the dill, garlic, and salt.
2. Pour the yogurt in and mix well.
3. Add cucumber, mint and stir well
4. Put inside the refrigerator to chill, then serve.

Nutrition:

- Calories: 167 kcal
- Carbs: 21g

- Fat: 4g
- Protein: 13g.

Grilled Steak and Sweet Potatoes

- ☐ Preparation Time: 10 minutes
- ☐ Cooking Time: 10 minutes
- ☐ Servings: 2

Ingredients:

- 8 oz. strip steak
- 1 Sweet potato
- 1 sliced onion
- ½ tsp. allspice
- ¼ tsp. cinnamon
- ¼ tsp. coriander
- ½ tsp. cumin
- ¼ tsp. cayenne pepper
- ½ tsp. ground ginger
- ½ tsp. salt
- 2 tsp. canola oil
- ½ tsp. grated orange zest

Directions:

1. Begin by preheating your grill to high.

2. In a medium bowl, combine the allspice, cinnamon, cayenne pepper, coriander, cumin, ginger, and salt. Next, you will want to sprinkle your steak with 2 ¼ teaspoons of the mixture.

3. Next, add the sweet potato and onion into the bowl and coat completely with the spice mixture.On a baking plate, add some foil on top and coat with cooking spray. You will want to layer the sweet potato mixture onto the tin foil and then fold the foil until you can pinch it together and seal the packet.You will want to place the packet on the hottest part of your grill and cook both sides for about 5 minutes.

4. On the same grill, cook your steaks for about 3 to 4 minutes on each side.For the final meal, serve the steak over the sweet potatoes, and your meal is complete.

Nutrition: Calories: 376g Protein: 34g Carbs: 16g Fat: 19g

Mediterranean Lamb Chops

- ☐ Preparation Time: 10 minutes
- ☐ Cooking Time: 10 minutes
- ☐ Servings: 4

Ingredients:

- 4 lamb shoulder chops, 8 ounce each
- 2 tablespoons Dijon mustard
- 2 tablespoons Balsamic vinegar
- 1 tablespoon garlic, chopped
- ½ cup olive oil
- 2 tablespoons shredded fresh basil

Directions:

1. Pat your lamb chop dry using a kitchen towel and arrange them on a shallow glass baking dish.
2. Take a bowl and whisk in Dijon mustard, balsamic vinegar, garlic, pepper, and mix well.
3. Whisk in the oil very slowly into the marinade until the mixture is smooth.Stir in basil.

4. Pour the marinade over the lamb chops and stir to coat both sides well. Cover the chops and allow them to marinate for 1-4 hours (chilled). Take the chops out and leave them for 30 minutes to allow the temperature to reach normal level.

5. Pre-heat your grill to medium heat and add oil to the grate.

6. Grill the lamb chops for 5-10 minutes per side until both sides are browned.

7. Once the center of the chop reads 145-degree Fahrenheit, the chops are ready, serve and enjoy!

Nutrition: Calories: 521g Fat: 45g Carbohydrates: 3.5g Protein: 22g

Broiled Mushrooms Burgers and Goat Cheese

- ☐ Preparation Time: 15 minutes
- ☐ Cooking Time: 5 minutes
- ☐ Servings: 4

Ingredients:

- 4 large Portobello mushroom caps
- 1 red onion, cut into ¼ inch thick slices
- 2 tablespoons extra virgin olive oil
- 2 tablespoons balsamic vinegar
- Pinch of salt
- ¼ cup goat cheese
- ¼ cup sun-dried tomatoes, chopped
- 4 ciabatta buns
- 1 cup kale, shredded

Directions:

1. Preheat your oven to broil.
2. Take a large bowl and add mushrooms caps, onion slices, olive oil, balsamic vinegar and salt.

3. Mix well.

4. Place mushroom caps (bottom side up) and onion slices on your baking sheet.

5. Take a small bowl and stir in goat cheese and sun-dried tomatoes.

6. Toast the buns under the broiler for 30 seconds until golden.

7. Spread the goat cheese mix on top of each bun.

8. Place mushroom cap and onion slice on each bun bottom and cover with shredded kale.

9. Put everything together and serve.

10. Enjoy!

Nutrition:

- Calories: 327 g Fat: 11g Carbohydrates: 49g Protein: 11g

Tuna and Potato Salad

- ☐ Preparation Time: 10 minutes
- ☐ Cooking Time: 0
- ☐ Servings: 4

Ingredients:

- 1 pound baby potatoes, scrubbed, boiled
- 1 cup tuna chunks, drained
- 1 cup cherry tomatoes, halved
- 1 cup medium onion, thinly sliced
- 8 pitted black olives
- 2 medium hard-boiled eggs, sliced
- 1 head Romaine lettuce
- Honey lemon mustard dressing
- ¼ cup olive oil
- 2 tablespoons lemon juice
- 1 tablespoon Dijon mustard
- 1 teaspoon dill weed, chopped
- Salt as needed
- Pepper as needed

Directions:

1. Take a small glass bowl and mix in your olive oil, honey, lemon juice, Dijon mustard and dill.

2. Season the mix with pepper and salt.Add in the tuna, baby potatoes, cherry tomatoes, red onion, green beans, black olives and toss. Everything nicely.

3. Arrange your lettuce leaves on a beautiful serving dish to make the base of your salad.

4. Top them with your salad mixture and place the egg slices. Drizzle it with the previously prepared Salad Dressing.

5. Serve hot.

Nutrition: Calories: 406 g Fat: 22g Carbohydrates: 28gProtein: 26g

Drinks Recipes

Almond Milk

- ☐ Preparation Time: 15 minutes, plus overnight to soak
- ☐ Cooking Time: 0 minutes
- ☐ Servings: 4

Ingredients:

- 2 cups raw unsalted almonds
- 4 cups water

Directions:

1. Place the almonds in a large bowl. Add enough water to cover them by 1 inch. Cover and let them sit at room temperature overnight.
2. The next day, drain the almonds and discard the water used to soak the almonds. Place the soaked almonds and the water in a blender and blend on high for several minutes until the mixture is opaque white.
3. Line a strainer with a double thickness of cheesecloth and place the strainer over a 2-quart bowl.
4. Pour the blended mixture into the strainer and let all the liquid drain off. Then gather the cheesecloth's edges and

twist to squeeze all the almond milk out of the cheesecloth. Discard the cheesecloth.

5. Flavor the almond milk however you'd like, and shake before serving.

6. Almond milk should be stored in an airtight container in the refrigerator and consumed within several days.

Tip: Almond milk can be left unflavored to use in savory dishes or for baking. For drinking, sweeten it slightly with 3 tablespoons of honey and 1 teaspoon of for the whole batch.

Nutrition:

- Calories: 40g
- Protein: 1g
- Total Carbohydrates: 2g
- Fiber: 1g
- Total Fat: 4g
- Saturated Fat: 0g,
- Cholesterol: 0mg Sodium: 140mg

Cranberry-Pumpkin Smoothie

☐ Preparation Time: 5 minutes

☐ Cooking Time: 0 minutes

☐ Servings: 2

Ingredients:

- 2 cups unsweetened almond milk
- 1 cup pure pumpkin purée
- ¼ cup gluten-free rolled oats
- ¼ cup pure cranberry juice (no sugar added)
- 1 tablespoon honey
- ¼ teaspoon ground cinnamon
- Pinch ground nutmeg

Directions:

1. In a blender, combine the almond milk, pumpkin, oats, cranberry juice, honey, cinnamon, and nutmeg and blend until smooth.
2. Pour into glasses and serve immediately.

Nutrition:

- Calories: 190g

- Total fat: 7g
- Saturated fat: 0g
- Carbohydrates: 26g
- Sugar: 12g
- Fiber: 5g
- Protein: 4g

Sweet Cranberry Nectar

- ☐ Preparation Time: 8 minutes
- ☐ Cooking Time: 5 minutes
- ☐ Servings: 4

Ingredients:

- 4 cups fresh cranberries
- 1 fresh lemon juice
- ½ cup agave nectar
- 1 piece of cinnamon stick
- 1 gallon water, filtered

Directions:

1. Add cranberries, ½ gallon water, and cinnamon into your pot
2. Close the lid
3. Cook on HIGH pressure for 8 minutes
4. Release the pressure naturally
5. Firstly, strain the liquid, then add remaining water
6. Cool, add agave nectar and lemon
7. Served chill and enjoy!

Nutrition:

- Calories: 184
- Fat: 0g
- Carbohydrates: 49g
- Protein: 1g

Raspberry Fizz Cocktail

☐ Preparation Time: 10 minutes

☐ Cooking Time: 0 minutes

☐ Servings: 4

Ingredients:

- 1 pint raspberries
- 2 tablespoons reduced-sugar raspberry jam
- 1 tablespoon lemon juice
- 2 teaspoons chopped fresh mint
- 1 bottle Prosecco, chilled

Directions:

1. Reserve 8 to 12 nice berries to float in wine glasses.
2. Place the remaining berries, raspberry jam, and lemon juice in a small bowl.
3. Using the back of a spoon or a pestle, mash the berries to release their juices and macerate them.
4. Place around 2 tablespoons of the mashed berries in each glass.
5. Add a pinch of chopped mint to each glass.

6. Gradually add the Prosecco, pouring slowly, so it doesn't overflow.

7. Stir once and serve.

Tip: You can crush the berries hours ahead or store the macerated berries in an ice cube tray in the freezer and use them frozen in this cocktail. If you can't find Prosecco in your area, any champagne or sparkling wine will work.

Nutrition:

- Calories: 204g Protein: 1g Total Carbohydrates: 18g
- Fiber: 5g Total Fat: 1g Saturated Fat: 0g
- Cholesterol: 0mg
- Sodium: 2mg

Chocolate Banana Smoothie

- ☐ Preparation Time: 5 minutes
- ☐ Cooking Time: 0 minutes
- ☐ Servings:2

Ingredients:

- 2 bananas, peeled
- 1 cup unsweetened almond milk, or skim milk
- 1 cup crushed ice
- 3 tablespoons unsweetened cocoa powder
- 3 tablespoons honey

Directions:

1. In a blender, combine the bananas, almond milk, ice, cocoa powder, and honey. Blend until smooth.

Nutrition:

- Calories: 219g
- Protein: 2g
- Total Carbohydrates: 57g
- Sugars: 40g
- Fiber: 6g

- Total Fat: 2g
- Saturated Fat: <1g
- Cholesterol: 0mg
- Sodium: 4mg

Fruit Smoothie

☐ Preparation Time: 5 minutes

☐ Cooking Time: 0 minutes Servings:2

Ingredients:

- 2 cups blueberries (or any fresh or frozen fruit, cut into pieces if the fruit is large)
- 2 cups unsweetened almond milk
- 1 cup crushed ice
- ½ teaspoon ground ginger (or other dried ground spice such as turmeric, cinnamon, or nutmeg)

Directions:

1. In a blender, combine the blueberries, almond milk, ice, and ginger. Blend until smooth.

Nutrition: Calories: 125g Protein: 2g Total Carbohydrates: 23g Sugars: 14g Fiber: 5g Total Fat: 4g Fat: <1g Cholesterol: 0mg Sodium: 181mg

Mangо-Pear Smoothie

- ☐ Preparation Time: 10 minutes
- ☐ Cooking Time: 0 minutes
- ☐ Servings: 1

Ingredients:

- 1 ripe pear, cored and chopped
- ½ mango, peeled, pitted, and chopped
- 1 cup chopped kale
- ½ cup plain Greek yogurt
- 2 ice cubes

Directions:

1. In a blender, purée the pear, mango, kale, and yogurt.
2. Add the ice and blend until thick and smooth. Pour the smoothie into a glass and serve cold.

Nutrition:

- Calories: 293g
- Total Fat: 8g
- Saturated Fat: 5g
- Carbohydrates: 53g

- Fiber: 7g
- Protein: 8g

CPSIA information can be obtained
at www.ICGtesting.com
Printed in the USA
LVHW081522120621
690063LV00003B/274